Without the Ten Commandments, Christians run a high risk of missing out on the best that God has to offer. We can swap God's joy for a series of spiritual kicks. We can lose God's freedom in orgies of self-indulgence. And we can mistake God's love for warm feelings in a cold world. The Ten Commandments cry out to be kept. They are God's signposts to his good life.

CHRISTIANITY

The Life That Pleases God

DAVID FIELD

LIVING BOOKS®
Tyndale House Publishers, Inc.
Wheaton, Illinois

*For Katie, with the prayer that she will live God's
good life as a citizen of the twenty-first century*

Living Books is a registered trademark of Tyndale House
Publishers, Inc.

First published under the title *God's Good Life* by InterVarsity
Press, Leicester, UK LE1 7GP. Living Books edition published in 1993 by Tyndale House Publishers, Inc.

Unless otherwise stated, Scripture quotations are from the
Holy Bible, New International Version. Copyright © 1973,
1978, 1984 by International Bible Society. Used by permis-
sion of Zondervan Bible Publishers. The *"NIV"* and *"New
International Version"* trademarks are registered in the
United States Patent and Trademark Office by International
Bible Society. Use of either trademark requires the permis-
sion of International Bible Society.

Scripture quotations marked TEV are from the *Good News
Bible,* Today's English Version, copyright © 1976 by American Bible Society.

Scripture quotations marked Phillips are from *The New Testament in Modern English,* translated by J. B. Phillips, copyright © 1958, 1959, 1960, 1972 by J. B. Phillips.

Library of Congress Catalog Card Number: 93-61453
ISBN:08423-1339-7

Printed in the United States of America

00 99 98 97 96 95 94
8   7   6   5   4   3   2   1

CONTENTS

PREFACE

A contractor's firm was busy demolishing a church building. The workmen had strict instructions to preserve anything of value. One of them noticed a stone slab with the Ten Commandments chiseled on it.

"Do we keep that?" he asked the foreman.

"No," said the foreman. "They don't use them these days."

He was right and he was wrong.

By and large, Christians do not spend much time on the Ten Commandments today. He was right about that.

Perhaps it is because these laws seem to reflect a picture of the Christian life that we do not find very attractive. In today's language, they are like ten heaven-to-earth missiles fired by a grim-faced God at his cowering people.

Where is the *love?* Where is the *freedom* Jesus promised to his followers? Where is the *joy* that lights up the pages of the New Testament so brilliantly?

I believe they are all there. In fact, I believe that without the Ten Commandments, Christians run a high risk of missing out on the best that God has to offer. We can swap God's joy for a series of spiritual kicks. We can lose God's freedom in orgies of self-indulgence. And we can mistake God's love for warm feelings in a cold world.

In the first part of this book, "Clearing the Ground," I have tried to face the critical questions honestly. Why are most of the Ten Commandments in the negative? Why do we need rules in the Christian life at all? And why should we rely on a set of regulations that sound so out of date?

If those questions do not interest you, I suggest you move straight on to chapter 3. From there on I hope you will see just how relevant the Ten Commandments are to modern life. Why does God get jealous? Can we become too intimate with the Lord who loves us? What should we be doing with our leisure time? How do we bridge the generation gap? What about issues of life and death, such as abortion and capital punishment? Why get married—and stay married?

What does our faith have to say about the way
we spend our money, use our tongues, and har-
ness our feelings?

It is a mouth-watering agenda. That demoli-
tion contractor's foreman was wrong after all.
The Ten Commandments cry out to be kept.
They are God's signposts to his good life.

This book has been on the boil for some time.
I am grateful to the governing body of Oak Hill
College for giving me time to write it. And I
want to say a special thank-you to Jo Bramwell
of IVP for her editing skills. The questions at the
end of each chapter are hers. Why not use them
to spark a discussion in a group with your
friends?

CLEARING THE GROUND

ONE
Accepting Rules

The Ten Commandments are a set of rules. No
one can get away from that. Even if they are not
printed with exclamation marks at the end of
each sentence, their clear aim is to tell us how
we ought and ought not to be living our lives.

Now that is controversial. Most people tolerate the laws of the land, but few of us get wildly
enthusiastic about keeping them. As a driver, I
see the sense of having rules that stop me from
being a menace to others on the road. But I find
speed limits very irritating when I am in a hurry.
And who really loves the sight of a traffic officer on patrol?

The thing that makes us hopping mad is when
the law pokes its nose into our private business.
Rules against murder and stealing seem fair
enough. But how strongly we resent it when law-

makers become baby-sitters. Nobody, surely, has the right to lay down the law about the way *I* relate to *my* parents or *my* sex partner!

Well, the Ten Commandments certainly claim that right. So before we get down to the specifics, we need to ask the hard questions. Is rule keeping good for us—or not?

Let's begin with the case for the opposition.

ARE RULES BAD FOR YOU?

A powerful case can be made for having as few rules in life as possible. Here are just some of the arguments used to convince us that rule keeping is—at best—a necessary evil.

Rules stifle your freedom. In the popular eye, Christianity is a policeman's religion. Obey the rules, and all will be well. Disobey just one, and you will feel God's heavy hand on your shoulder.

Joy Davidman describes this image superbly at the beginning of her book, *Smoke on the Mountain.* She tells the story of a Western missionary (of the pith-helmet-under-the-palm-tree variety) doing his best to convert an old African chief by using the Ten Commandments.

> "I do not understand," said the chief at last.
> "You tell me that I must not take my neighbor's wife?"

"That's right," said the missionary.

"Or his ivory, or his oxen?"

"Quite right."

"And I must not dance the war dance and then ambush him on the trail and kill him?"

"Absolutely right!"

"But I cannot do any of these things!" said the chief regretfully. "I am too old. To be old and to be a Christian, they are the same thing!"

How many people, Miss Davidman concludes, picture Christianity as something old, sapless, joyless, mumbling in the corner, casting sour looks at the young people's fun? How many unconsciously conceive of God as rather like the famous old lady who said, "Find out what the baby's doing and make him stop"?

How many, we might add, pity Christians as rule-bound freaks, men and women who have surrendered their human freedom and now edge their way painfully through life tied up by yards and yards of religious red tape?

Christians protest that this is an unfair caricature. But how can we escape it if we insist on taking the Ten Commandments seriously as our Christian rule book?

We need standards, not rules. Throwing away rules is not at all the same thing as having no standards or values in life.

Most people who refuse to be bound by rules turn out to have their own jealously guarded personal moral values. The terrorist who plants a bomb at an airport terminal may be an ardent Red Cross supporter. And the thief who steals your car may be carrying a kidney donor card.

People like this are not against having standards as such. They simply object to the codifying of those standards in a rule book that demands wooden obedience from everyone forever. They refuse to toe other people's lines.

In June 1991, a British RAF officer was convicted, by a court-martial, of negligence. He had left three cases and a laptop computer containing classified secrets about the Gulf War in his car while he looked round a secondhand car showroom. In his absence, the cases were stolen. Fortunately for him, the precious items were returned intact. With them came a note from the man who had taken them. It read, "I am a common thief. I'm also a patriot and I love my queen and country. Whoever lost this should be bloody hung."

There spoke a lawbreaker who had his standards. And if that attempt to seize the moral high ground at the expense of rules leaves you unconvinced, think about a more famous thief.

In English folklore, no star shines more brightly than Robin Hood. Robin was the prototype of a guerrilla freedom-fighter. From the comparative safety of Sherwood Forest, he carried out daring raids against wealthy authority figures in order to feed and clothe their downtrodden victims.

Unfortunately, there was just one ethical snag about the way he operated. In order to achieve his goals, Robin stole.

But who cares about that? *Who cares* whether a man with the guts of a rebel ignores a moral and legal veto like "You shall not steal" in order to redistribute wealth in the interest of justice? Robin Hood brought a lot of poor people a great deal of happiness, while his wealthy victims hardly missed their losses. He put principles before rules. In a way, he did illegally what the tax collector enforces today by law, taking money from the richer to provide assistance for the poorer members of the community.

We need more Robin Hoods who are prepared to tear up the rule book in order to express values in life that really matter. That is the argument. It is our standards that are important. Rules and regulations are just diversions.

Rules stop you from making up your own mind. Keeping rules turns people into robots. That is another charge. There may be a case for telling young children what they must and must not do. They may damage themselves otherwise. But mature adults can be trusted to find their own way through life's moral maze.

How do we make up our minds when we are faced with a tough moral choice? Not by running to the rule book for a preset answer. That is kids' stuff! As grown-up people, our responsibility is to weigh the alternatives and calculate how much good or harm our actions may cause. If something I plan to do will hurt other people, it has to be wrong. But if it does no one any harm (or does more good than harm), it surely must be right—whatever the rule books say.

Toward the end of the Second World War, a German woman named Mrs. Bergmeier was captured by the advancing Russian army and taken off to a prison camp. News reached her that her husband and three children badly needed her in Berlin. The only way out of the camp, she discovered, was to get pregnant. After weighing the pros and cons very carefully, she asked a friendly guard to have sex with her. He obliged; she was released when her pregnancy was confirmed, and the new baby was welcomed with great delight into the reunited family.

Yes, Mrs. Bergmeier had broken one of the Ten Commandments. But her act of adultery was justified by the results. So argues Professor Joseph Fletcher, who tells her story.

Rules leave no room for love. Joseph Fletcher wrote an influential book in the 1960s called *Situation Ethics*. In it he suggested that Christians should use love, not rules, as their guideline. After all, didn't Jesus sum up all the regulations in the Old Testament rule book by saying, "You shall *love* God. . . . You shall *love* your neighbor as yourself"?

What really matters, Fletcher insisted, is not whether you obey a rule but whether your heart is in the right place. Love is Christ's antidote to the Ten Commandments. Providing you think, talk, and act in a loving way, you cannot possibly go wrong.

If, on the other hand, you grimly insist on keeping all the rules, even though it is sometimes unloving to do so, you turn yourself into "good people in the worst sense of the word," to use Mark Twain's telling phrase. And if you go on living that way, how can you possibly escape the sharp criticisms Jesus aimed at the champion rule keepers of his time—the Pharisees?

We can't trust the people who make and enforce the rules. Here is the knockout blow. The main reason why rule keeping gets such bad press

today is that the rule makers and rule enforcers
have lost their credibility.

Most of us are fairly cynical about the authority
figures we know. When a politician smiles
blandly at us from the television screen, we find
ourselves automatically hunting for the half-truths
and deceptions behind the persuasive words.

It is the same in all departments of life. A camera captures a policeman dealing violently with a
demonstrator, and we begin to wonder whether all
policemen abuse their authority. When a doctor
faces the courts, charged with sexually abusing a
patient, vague doubts creep into our minds about
the wisdom of sending our daughters to the doctor's office on their own. A bishop runs off to the
Bahamas with someone else's wife, and bang
goes the last vestige of our faith in the church as
the nation's conscience. Is nothing sacred?

ARE RULES GOOD FOR YOU?

There, in a nutshell, is the case against the rule
book. Rule keeping robs you of your freedom,
blinds you to life's really important values and
standards, turns you into an unthinking robot,
and makes you coldly unloving in the way you
deal with human need. And we simply cannot
trust those who make and enforce the regulations.

What is there to be said on the other side? Well, plenty!

Rules safeguard your freedom. It seems obvious that rules *restrict* freedom. How can they possibly safeguard it?

Everything depends on the way you define *freedom*. If you think first of being free *from* things, rules are irritating intrusions into your personal liberty. But if you focus instead on freedom *for* living a satisfying life, a few well-chosen rules can do a lot to enhance your prospects.

I know a minister of a church in a wealthy suburban area. Most of the people he serves are delightfully free from the restrictions that money (I mean the lack of it) imposes on the rest of us. My friend has a job keeping up with the latest status symbols. His parishioners are well past their second swimming pool.

But are they really free? He tells me that a home visit to a church member has to be planned like a military operation. First the electronic surveillance devices on the gate at the end of the drive have to be negotiated. Then he dares not get out of his car outside the front door until someone arrives to restrain the guard dogs. It's all in the interest of security, of course—so the people inside their self-made garrison can "enjoy" their possessions without becoming the victims of thieves.

I also know a small village four hundred miles away where the atmosphere is totally different. The people there enjoy what they have, though they don't have very much. But the feature of village life that used to astonish me is that most of them leave the keys in their front doors when they go out. And their cars stay unlocked. In that small, untypical community, the need for security is not so great because theft is less of a problem.

Given the choice, I know where I would prefer to live as a free man. In a society where men and women observe the eighth commandment ("You shall not steal"), personal liberty is enhanced, not diminished.

Rules make social life possible. It is all very well to say that we do not need rules, so long as we hang on to our standards and values. But chaos reigns when individuals are allowed to express their personal sets of values unchecked.

The man who stole the RAF officer's cases and computer—but then returned the classified information when he might have sold it for a lot of money—was being very selective in the moral standards he championed. He valued patriotism very highly, but honesty hardly at all.

Many terrorists are keen patriots, too. The Irish Republican Army bomb maker has his standards. But few would agree with him that he has a moral right to blow up an army band in a London park (along with the audience), just because he must be allowed to express his personal values freely. If we are to live together safely in a caring community, we need firm laws against homicide as well as theft.

This is really only an extension of the previous point. Legal restrictions actually increase our liberty rather than ruin it. I live in a smokeless zone. That stops me from lighting an ordinary coal fire in my house—but it also means I can breathe more freely. The law also stops me from discriminating against people from other ethnic groups—but the end result is that they and I can enjoy greater freedom in living together.

God's rules help us make up our minds. God did not make human beings as unthinking robots. He gave us minds and he means us to reason our way through to conclusions sensibly. The New Testament urges us, "Be transformed by the renewing of your mind. Then you will be able to test and approve what God's will is" (Romans 12:2).

All the same, words such as *transform* and

renew ring loud warning bells. As ordinary people, our minds are fallible. Without God's renewing, transforming help, we can so easily reason our way to *wrong* conclusions. And God does give us the help we need—in the shape of his law, as well as in other ways. As we shall see, the Ten Commandments do not answer all of our questions neatly. But they do provide a solid framework within which we can use our Christian minds to work out right solutions to life's problems.

It is simply not good enough to say, "I will throw away God's rule book and work out for myself the course of action that will cause the least harm and do the most good." Predicting the weather is easy, compared with forecasting the results of the things we do.

It is not usually so hard to decide whether a course of action will lead to disaster in five minutes' time—or even next week. But the farther we peer into the future, the less reliable our forecasting becomes. We only have to look back into our personal pasts to be reminded of that. If only I had *known* that last year's thoughtless conversation would wreck such a precious relationship now . . . but how could I possibly have guessed?

God, of course, is the only fail-safe long-range forecaster in the business. Only he can see clearly over our short-term horizons. And one highly beneficial consequence of keeping his rules is that they protect us from making long-term mistakes.

Jesus made this point very simply when he told his story of the two builders (see Matthew 7:24-27). The man who took a shortcut by ignoring the basic rules in his building manual was the long-term loser. Exactly the same would happen, Jesus warned, to anyone "who hears these words of mine and does not put them into practice."

Long ago (so long that they cannot be identified now), I knew two Christian couples who discovered this truth in a way that surprised them. Outwardly, their marriages were stable and happy. But one husband fell in love with the other man's wife. She found him very attractive, too.

A touch led to a hug and a hug to a kiss. You can guess the rest. They stopped short of intercourse—just—until one evening they discussed the possibility openly and (as they thought) weighed all the pros and cons sensibly. They even prayed about it. Their conclusion was clear. It would be all right for them to have sex. They were sure God would rubber-stamp their decision. It seemed the most loving thing to do. But they never did it. They were held back by the words of the seventh commandment, "You shall *not* commit adultery."

At the time it was a frustrating irritation to them. But later, with the wisdom of hindsight, they told me how grateful they were that God's rule had stopped them in their tracks. The long-term consequences for their children, for their jobs, and for themselves would have been horren-dous. Why did they not see that at the time? Per-haps just because they were human and fallible.

GOD'S RULES SHAKE US OUT OF OUR COMPLACENCY

It is one thing to *know* that something is wrong, but quite another to *feel* ashamed and to *resolve to change.* Here, too, the Ten Commandments have an important role to play.

During one of Billy Graham's evangelistic campaigns, a student went forward in response to the "Get up out of your seats" appeal at the end of an evening meeting. But he did not want to become a Christian. He collected autographs and wanted to add Billy's scalp to his list. Slip-ping past his counselor neatly, he made for the great man and asked for his signature. Billy obliged with a smile.

On his way back home the young man decided that Billy Graham did not merit a place in his collection after all, so he tore the page out of his book and threw it away. But something the evangelist had said during the meeting stuck in his mind. He had described the Ten Commandments as a mirror that shows us up for the people we really are.

The student decided to conduct his own test. He bought a secondhand Bible at a cut-rate price, found the Ten Commandments, tore the page out, and stuck it to his bathroom mirror. After living with God's rules for a week, he went back to the Billy Graham campaign fully convinced of his need for God's pardon. He went forward again, but not to get an autograph.

Centuries earlier, Paul confessed to a similar experience. "I should never have felt guilty of the sin of coveting," he wrote, "if I had not heard the Law saying, 'Thou shalt not covet.'" And he went on to add a refreshingly honest postscript: "But the sin in me, finding in the commandment an opportunity to express itself, stimulated all my desires" (Romans 7:7-8, Phillips).

God's rules have this curious double effect. If they do not drive us back to God in a search for his pardon, they make forbidden things doubly attractive. If there is a notice saying No Entry, we automatically open the door to see what is on the other side. If a book is banned, its sales soar.

This tendency in human nature (and it is more perverse than simple curiosity) underlines our spiritual and moral helplessness. To use Paul's word picture, "The law was put in charge to lead us to Christ" (Galatians 3:24). It exposes our impotence to live a life that squares with God's standards, and it stimulates our desire to sin even more than we otherwise would. And it does not let us rest until it has led us to Jesus to find God's forgiveness and strength.

We need God's rules to shake us out of our moral complacency. And that need does not end once we have given our lives to Christ as Savior and Lord. There is no such thing as instant perfection in the Christian life. The Ten Commandments are the Holy Spirit's spur to goad the Christian conscience to a more and more realistic discipleship until, in Spurgeon's words, "it should shiver when even the ghost of a sin goes by."

God's law provides love with solid backbone. "Love, and do what you like," writes Joseph Fletcher, quoting St. Augustine (who actually meant something a little different). That sounds very much like a Christian sentiment. What can possibly be wrong with it?

Rather more than meets the eye! Letting love guide all our decisions sounds fine—so long as we are absolutely clear what love means. But the dice are loaded heavily against us if we try to find a clear definition. In our culture, *love* can mean anything from going to bed with someone you fancy ("I make love") to treating a pet affectionately ("I love my kitten") or enjoying the food and scenery on holiday ("I love escargot"). Claiming love as your guideline is rather like draping your car with Christmas tree lights, removing the headlights, and setting off down the freeway at night in a fog.

Jesus certainly put love right at the top of his list of Christian responsibilities. He also defined it in terms of *attitude* rather than emotion (so even enemies can be loved). But he never drew the conclusion that Joseph Fletcher draws—that a loving motive replaces the need to obey rules in the Christian life.

Quite the reverse. "Do not think," said Jesus, "that I have come to abolish the Law or the Prophets; I have not come to abolish them but to fulfill them. . . . Anyone who breaks one of the least of these commandments and teaches others to do the same will be called least in the kingdom of heaven" (Matthew 5:17, 19).

There is no hint there that Christians are meant to choose between obeying the Ten Commandments and following the way of love. Jesus did not intend to replace the Old Testament law when he summed it up in his two famous love commandments. His aim was to remind his hearers (especially those who were legalistically minded) that love is the headline over the small print. His formula was both/and, not either/or. In his teaching, love brings to law a new warmth and law provides love with sturdy backbone.

We have a Rule Maker we can trust. At the heart of our dislike of rules is a mistrust of the people who make and enforce them. There are so many things in ordinary life that make us deeply suspicious of authority figures—all those men and women (and they are mainly men) who are only too keen to tell us what we should or should not be doing.

We know pigheaded husbands who use their muscle to turn their homes into chauvinist sties. We read about children who are physically abused by their fathers. We suffer at the hands of politicians who exercise their power to advance their own careers. We see all around us the evidence of human selfishness reducing the environment to a shambles. And when we focus on *that* kind of thing, the mere mention of authority leaves us feeling distinctly fidgety.

Is this perhaps why the Ten Commandments have fallen out of favor today? It is certainly hard to miss the note of authority behind them. When God gave these rules to Moses, he laid on an awesome set of audiovisual phenomena to underline the fact that he was in charge. Thunder, lightning, earthquake, and trumpet blast all left the people trembling with fear at the foot of the mountain. It was a mind-blowing show of power, a sound-and-light display that had the single, simple aim of stimulating submission to the Lawgiver's authority.

God certainly has every right to demand our obedience. He also has the power to enforce it. But that alone does not fully satisfy us. Might is not always right. If God were simply a souped-up Saddam Hussein with a super-nuclear capacity, our obedience to his laws would be less than wholehearted.

But that, of course, is not at all what God is like. As we shall see in chapter 3, he gave his people the Ten Commandments out of sheer love, not from a desire to impose his authority by force. Unlike any human nursemaid, he really does know how human life can be lived at its best. And that makes submission to his authority exciting as well as rewarding. In a word, we can trust the divine Rule Maker.

God's laws *are* good for you. That is the message of the whole Bible. It may grate on modern ears tuned to the blandishments of a permissive society, but it is time modern Christians shouted it from the public-address systems without embarrassment.

We could do much worse than echo John Wesley's bold words: "I cannot spare the law one moment, no more than I can spare Christ; seeing I now want it as much, to keep me to Christ, as ever I wanted it to bring me to Him. . . . Indeed, each is continually sending me to the other, the law to Christ, and Christ to the law."

TO THINK AND TALK ABOUT

1. Do rules stifle freedom, or safeguard it? How do you arrive at your answer?

2. "Keeping rules turns people into robots. . . . Mature adults can be trusted to find their own way through life's moral maze." Say why you would agree or disagree.

3. Let some members of your group form a collective "Joseph Fletcher." "Joseph" kicks off the discussion by maintaining that love, not rules, must be our guide. Argue it through as a group, bearing in mind the points the author makes in the section entitled "Are Rules Good for You?"

4. What is good about feeling guilty?

5. Why do we get so uptight about authority figures? What is different about God's authority?

TWO
Ancient and Modern

A cartoonist drew two British businessmen, immaculate in their pin-striped trousers and bowler hats, leaning against a bar. "What we need," one is solemnly telling the other, "is a strong, authoritarian government with the courage to bring in compulsory *laissez-faire.*"

That piece of fun aptly illustrates the tension I have been trying to describe in chapter 1. We live in an age that mocks authority and is angered by rules. We demand to be allowed to do our own thing. But at the same time we clamor for strong government and for laws that are properly enforced. It is a curious piece of doublethink.

The Christian's response is to point to God and the Ten Commandments. God alone has a loving authority that is beyond challenge. And his rules for life leave no room for any ifs or buts. We can never take him to arbitration.

But we have not yet got quite to the heart of the uneasiness many people (including some Christians) feel about using the Ten Commandments today. Most people would go along with the idea that life needs a set of good rules if we are not going to live in a permanent state of civil war. All Christians would go a step farther and agree that God has the authority to tell us what to do. But are the Ten Commandments God's guideline for life *at the end of the twentieth century?* That is the key question.

ANCIENT AND OUTDATED?
Some honestly believe that the Ten Commandments have had their day. They deserve a place of honor in a museum of biblical antiquities, but to take them seriously as God's rules for modern life would be the equivalent of using an out-of-date medical textbook as our main weapon in fighting cancer. God surely means us to do better than that.

There is plenty of evidence to support this point of view.

The tone of the Ten Commandments seems out of tune with modern attitudes. The story is told of Winston Churchill's first day at a new school.

He was ordered to do a Latin exercise. "Why?" he asked in all innocence.

There was a shocked silence. "Because I told you to do it!" the furious teacher finally spluttered.

Young Winston was ahead of his time. Today's children are encouraged, at home as well as at school, to ask questions and to make experiments. If they are told to do something, they expect a good answer to the question *why?* It is far better not to force them to do anything at all, parents are advised, because everyone learns best from making his own mistakes.

The Ten Commandments are certainly out of tune with this shift in educational policy. There are no explanations in the margin to make their demands sound more reasonable to modern ears. *Why* is it so wrong to have sex outside marriage if it does no one any harm? *Why* must a father who has sexually abused his daughter be "honored" by her? *Why* should we work a six-day week? We really want to hear the reasons. But the Ten Commandments do not offer us any at all.

Worse still, all but two of them are expressed in the negative. They are not so much commandments as prohibitions.

Modern psychology stresses the importance of being positive. Repressed desires lead straight to psychological sickness. The root of repression, the specialists tell us, is often to be found in infancy when the young child was caged in by a frustrating chorus of adult don'ts. So the old practice of teaching children to learn the Ten Commandments by heart adds up to a serious health risk. The negative attitude to life they encourage is as dangerous as exposure to meningitis or diphtheria. At least that is the conclusion we are invited to draw.

A negative attitude to sex is one of the most frequently heard accusations laid at the church's door. If "You shall not commit adultery" is the only guideline the young Christian has in directing his or her sex life, damaging repression is surely only just around the corner. That was certainly Bertrand Russell's opinion when he wrote luridly about the need to "cleanse sex from the filth with which it has been covered by Christian moralists."

The Ten Commandments ignore the social dimension of our behavior. One evening I found myself at a table in a café with two strangers, drinking coffee. We had been to the same Christian meeting, listening to an evangelist, and they were discussing the talk. "That guy was right," one of them said. "We're far from perfect. If there is a God, we need him to forgive us."

"Sure," replied the other, "but whose fault is it that we're the way we are? I blame this {****} society that we live in."

I doubt whether either of them knew much about the Marxist analysis, though I may be misjudging them, but Marxist socialism has been very influential in switching our attention from the personal to the collective. Individually, we are the helpless victims of the standards and values rammed down our throats by our social environment. That's the theory, anyway. Don't blame me—blame it.

Personal moral standards have become a matter of personal preference. So if a cinema puts on a film that features homosexual lovemaking, no one minds. But the manager is a fool if he shows a movie advocating racism. That is a sure way to get his seats ripped and his screen slashed. Racism is a corrupt social structure, trapping both the oppressors and their victims. No one can afford to be permissive about a social evil like that.

Seen against this modern background, the Ten Commandments look decidedly dated. The repeated *thou* in the older version gives the game away. Their target is personal behavior, and on that they sound impossibly inflexible and intolerant. But when it comes to structural sin, they have nothing to say at all. The burning social, cultural, and economic issues that grab the headlines in today's tabloids are simply ignored.

The Ten Commandments are preoccupied with irrelevancies. This is really an extension of the last point. The charge is that the Ten Commandments are not just out-of-date because they focus on personal behavior. Even the *kind* of personal behavior they highlight sounds rather quaint and queer.

Not many people in a modern society, for example, are tempted to make idols in their garden sheds. And the Sabbath commandment (which was, of course, intended to regulate behavior on Saturday, not Sunday) is hardly relevant when it gets down to the details. Very few of us have a manservant or maidservant, let alone an alien within our gates.

The most powerful reading of the Ten Commandments I have ever heard took place in a tiny Welsh village church during a service of Holy Communion. When the minister got to the tenth (the one about coveting), he paused after each item and glared fiercely at different members of his congregation. I could imagine the well-dressed man in the front row shuffling uncomfortably as he felt the rector's eyes on him when he got to "maidservant." And I could feel the farmer at the back positively wilting during the pregnant pause after "ox."

That all happened many years ago. But the fact that it has stuck in my memory for so long underlines how unusual it is to hear the Ten Commandments strike home with such contemporary relevance. Back in the sixteenth century, Richard Hooker wrote, "The Decalogue of Moses declareth summarily those things that we ought to do." Queen Elizabeth I ordered that copies should be placed in all churches. The Anglican *Book of Common Prayer* instructed godparents to make sure that the youngsters they sponsored learned the Ten Commandments by heart. But today these Old Testament regulations have a much lower profile in most of our church teaching programs.

It is not just that their wording sounds old-fashioned. As directives for modern life, they do not tackle some of the moral problems that trouble our consciences most. If this is really God's rule book for the late twentieth century, it leaves some huge gaps between the lines.

Not long ago, the British parliament debated the morality of experimenting on the human embryo. Members were allowed a free vote. Christians spoke out in the discussion. But no one mentioned the Ten Commandments, as far as I know. And why should they? Why should a code written thousands of years ago be expected to give definitive guidance on modern medical procedures? Even the command "You shall not murder" was not obviously relevant when the main point of dispute was the status of a human embryo less than fourteen days old.

The Ten Commandments do not recognize the complexity of decision making. Sometimes the demand of one commandment appears to clash with another. In some societies, for example, there is a conflict between the instruction to honor a parent (the fifth commandment) and the veto on taking a life (the sixth).

In some parts of China, victims of senile dementia are taken down to the river and drowned. That is not perceived as a callous act on the part of adult children who cannot or will not care for their elderly parents. It is seen as an act of mercy to prevent old people from dying without dignity. It is easy to see the connection between that ancient practice and the increasing demands for euthanasia in Western society today.

Even in the Bible itself, there are examples of one commandment being set aside in the interests of another. Shortly before Jericho's walls came tumbling down, Rahab the prostitute found herself with an awkward moral choice to make. The town's secret police asked her if she knew the whereabouts of two Israelite spies. She had just hidden them on the roof of her house, but to save their lives she told a lie—and is commended for it in the New Testament (see Joshua 2 and James 2:25).

It would be easy to multiply the examples. The problem with the Ten Commandments, say the critics, is that they make blunt demands without exceptions. It might be nice to obey all of them all of the time. But life is not like that. Sometimes we have to break one in order to keep another. Sometimes there is an overriding concern that justifies our disobedience. And at all times we must be tolerant when other people breach this ancient law code in order to do (what they think) is the right thing.

ANCIENT AND RELEVANT?

Those are the charges. I hope I have been fair to the people who make them. But I confess that my tongue has been in my cheek as I have run through the list, because I find the case they make far from convincing. It is my firm and honest conviction that the Ten Commandments are as relevant today as they were on the awesome day Moses received them.

Here are just five reasons why we should take these commandments seriously as God's guidelines for modern living.

First, the Ten Commandments recall us to God's pattern for living. Among the junk mail that arrived on my doormat one morning was a fascinating pamphlet advertising a set of morality tales for children. "Teach your children how 'old-fashioned' values are more vital today than ever," it proclaimed. "In short, the kind of yesterday values that every caring adult likes to see in today's children."

Why fascinating? Well, it might have been a plug for a series of books about the Ten Commandments. The contents certainly matched. But it was actually nothing of the kind. It came from a secular source, without any shred of a suggestion that the values it endorsed so boldly reflected the set of rules God gave his people thousands of years ago. Somewhere, some hardnosed editor in a publishing firm had decided that enough modern parents would find "yesterday values" helpful in training their children to make this new series a commercial success.

Christians should not be surprised at that. The Ten Commandments keep their relevance because they continue to provide what today's children (and, one might add, today's adults as well) really need. To put it crudely, they scratch where ordinary people itch. The man on the street is against murder, theft, deceit, and greed, just as he is in favor of stable family life and a balance between work and leisure, even though he never goes to church.

Why should this be? The Bible has its own solution. "The requirements of [God's] law," explains Paul, "are written on their hearts" (Romans 2:15). He was referring to men and women who had never read the Ten Commandments. Ordinary people like that, he maintained, just *know*—because they are human—that God's law makes good sense. Even the atheist cannot eradicate this writing on his heart. It is the indelible mark on his human personality of the God he does not believe in.

Christians do not have a monopoly on conscience. That is Paul's point. The most determined nonreader of the Bible feels twinges of guilt when she tells a lie or goes to bed with someone else's husband (for the first few times, anyway). And the reason lies in the way she is made. The built-in standards and values that tweak her conscience come from the God she rejects.

Perhaps this lay behind the embarrassment of an anonymous psychiatrist who cares for AIDS patients, when he was asked by a journalist, "If we had played by New Testament rules on sexual behavior, would we have ever had an epidemic?" "Of course not," replied the specialist, "but for God's sake don't quote me on that!"

For many years now, scholars have pointed

out how closely the Ten Commandments reflect God's plan for human life set out in the Bible's teaching about creation. They almost read like an action replay of the life-style the Creator intended for human beings—a life characterized by God-centeredness, balance between work and leisure, faithful relationships, and respect for others. No wonder anthropologists detect echoes of this pattern in communities and cultures all over the world.

Second, the Ten Commandments get to the heart of human nature. The big difference, of course, between the Bible's creation teaching and the Ten Commandments is the way they are phrased. The Creator's plan in Genesis is set out as a positive statement. God's law in Exodus (where the Ten Commandments first appear) swaps the periods for exclamation marks and adds the negative "You shall nots." Why is that?

Again, the reason takes us right to the heart of human nature. Man and woman have rebelled against their Creator. While acknowledging the good sense of his pattern for life, they resist conforming to it. Just knowing about it is no longer enough. We have to be *told* firmly to *obey* in the language of *law*—or we know we will declare and do the other thing.

Our fingers itch over the self-destruct button.

Given half a chance, we stupidly choose to ruin our relationships with God, with others, and with our environment. We abuse our Creator, become workaholics, break marriages, ignore parents, devalue life, and cheat other people. "For *out of the heart*," commented Jesus, "come evil thoughts, murder, adultery, sexual immorality, theft, false testimony, slander" (Matthew 15:19, emphasis mine).

We badly need a set of fences with prominently displayed danger signals if we are not to push each other over the edge of life's cliffs. The Ten Commandments are those fences. God will not stop us from climbing over them, but he did love us enough to put them up.

This is realism, not pessimism. Some well-meaning people try to persuade us that we should drop all the negatives and substitute the simple encouragement to "live a life of love." That sounds fine, but it is not in tune with the Bible. Even the best-known New Testament passage on love, 1 Corinthians 13, bristles with negatives. Love "does not envy, it does not boast, it is not proud. It is not rude, it is not self-seeking, it is not easily angered, it keeps no record of wrongs" (verses 4 and 5). The positives are there as well, but even the law of love needs warning fences if we are not to abuse it.

The Ten Commandments are relevant because

they speak to us as we really are. They call us to the kind of life we are made to live. But they do not treat us as though we have just stepped out of stained-glass windows.

Third, the Ten Commandments reach to the roots of society's problems. Those who complain that the Ten Commandments ignore social issues have misunderstood their radical nature.

They are certainly aimed at the individual. No one who reads them can escape from personal responsibility by pleading, "Blame my society, not me." But the singular *you* refers to the whole community, too.

That is how we are to understand the mysterious tailpiece after the command to "honor your father and your mother." The suggestion seems to be that individual sons and daughters who respect their parents will live to a ripe old age— which does not always happen, of course. But there is a far more profound truth at the community level here.

The commandment is, in fact, making a very bold social statement. The claim is that a society that maintains the structures of family life in a healthy state will enjoy stability. It also implies that the days of a society that ignores family values are numbered. That is certainly a controversial assertion, but as a contribution to the general debate about social values, it demands serious attention.

Even more radically, this link the Ten Commandments forges between the behavior of individuals and the health of society traces social problems to their roots in human nature. The Marxist says, "Put the structures of society right, and all problems at the personal level will melt away." The Bible retorts, never more clearly than here in the Ten Commandments, "Get people's attitudes and behavior right, and bad social structures will be challenged and changed."

Jesus sought to bring individual men and women into full commitment to God, knowing that genuine faith would lead to far-reaching social consequences. And history amply illustrates how religious conversion does in fact bring a new social alertness, as well as changing personal life-styles. Periods of revival in religious faith have usually been followed by periods of beneficial social change.

All this is very much in keeping with the style of the Ten Commandments. Their social, economic, and political impact is enormous. When the president of the United States of America places his hand on a copy of the Scriptures containing these commandments as he takes the oath at his inauguration ceremony, he is doing something far more significant than giving a respectful nod to tradition.

Fourth, the Ten Commandments leave plenty of room for decision making. Several paragraphs ago, I compared the Ten Commandments to a set of fences, warning us against the "no go" areas of life. Others see them in a much less flattering light—more as a pattern of depth charges, which turn life in our little human submarines into a frightening business of dodging disasters constantly threatened from above.

I want to stay with my word picture. A fence on the edge of a cliff is not threatening. It restricts your freedom to do something stupid (if you take any notice of it), but your liberty to walk the cliff path is not affected. It might even make your day—and your holiday—if it stops you from finishing up in the hospital or the mortuary.

The Ten Commandments are not wishy-washy generalizations. They are clear, pointed, and personal. But they are not fussy. They cover an enormous amount of ground, but they are not comprehensive. They sometimes illustrate their point by making specific allusions (to servants and donkeys, for example), but they do not collapse into a detailed list of bylaws that tell you what you must do—or stop doing—in every conceivable situation.

Some people see that as a fault. What use,
they ask, is a set of headlines without the small
print? How do we know if it is right for an
engaged couple to do more than cuddle and kiss
if our only guideline is "You shall not commit
adultery"? How much more useful, mused the
legalists of Jesus' time, to unpack the simple
Sabbath commandment in thirty-four volumes
that spell out what "not working" actually
means. So they did exactly that—and earned
Jesus' scalding criticism for doing so.

The Pharisees displayed the depth-charge
mentality. It is totally alien to the spirit of the
Ten Commandments. The advantage of a code
that lists the headlines only is that it stays relevant. It allows people of different cultures to
write in their own small print, without kidding
themselves that in doing so they are saying
God's last word for everyone else. And the
beauty of a simple code that leans heavily on
"you shall nots" is that it leaves people with
loads of space in which to decide what they
should be doing.

*Fifth, the Ten Commandments are clear about
essentials.* Letters to *The Times* can be quite
complex and mind testing. The one I remember
best was neither. It formed the postscript to a
lengthy exchange of correspondence about a

hotly disputed issue of theology. "Sir," began this refreshing little note, "may we please have a little less theological codswallop and lot more 'Thus says the Lord'?"

The Ten Commandments do not go into claustrophobic detail, but they are crystal clear on essentials. There is no hint of any tolerance toward those who would prefer to debate the few things that are laid down flat.

Most of us live in societies that prize tolerance. We are encouraged to approach matters like committing adultery and keeping Sabbaths in a "Do you take sugar?" frame of mind. You may or you may not do as I do, but we will not think any the worse of each other for that, will we?

Tolerance is the logical outcome of relativism. Relativists are people who believe that there are no moral rules that apply to everyone everywhere. What is right and wrong depends on who you are and where you live. So we must all be tolerant.

There can be no marriage between relativism and the Ten Commandments. They are totally incompatible. The Bible itself recognizes that on rare occasions we may be faced with the awful choice of breaking one commandment in order to keep another. We may have to tell a lie to save a life. But if we take the Ten Commandments seriously we will not see such situations as the relativist sees them.

William Barclay illustrates the difference like this. Imagine, he says, that you have a dangerous drug in your medicine cabinet. The Ten Commandments mentality encourages you to label that bottle POISON in large letters, to warn you of the danger you face whenever you have to use it. The relativist tears the label off.

Very, very occasionally, it may be necessary to break a commandment. But the need to make that kind of decision should bring tears to your eyes. It is a far more serious matter than deciding—for once—not to take sugar in your coffee.

Ancient? Yes, very. The Ten Commandments have their roots deep in Old Testament history. But they are refreshingly modern, too. They remind us of the way our Creator means for us to live. They treat us as the mixed-up people we really are, not as plaster-cast saints. They are more radical than many modern politicians, getting to the roots of social issues. And they are crystal clear about essentials, while giving us freedom to sort out the details of life for ourselves.

TO THINK AND TALK ABOUT

1. Why do you think "yesterday values" still appeal to people brought up on "modern attitudes"?

2. The Ten Commandments focus on *personal* behavior in an ancient culture. Does this mean they have nothing to say about today's *social* evils? Explain your answer.

3. "The Ten Commandments are too simplistic," says your friend. "We can't base our complex modern lives on them." How would you reply?

4. "On rare occasions we may be faced with the awful choice of breaking one commandment in order to keep another." Do you agree? Why or why not? What is the distinction between this position and that of the relativist?

THE TEN COMMANDMENTS

THREE
Two-Way Commitment: The First Commandment

And God spoke all these words:
 "I am the LORD your God, who brought you out of Egypt, out of the land of slavery.
 "You shall have no other gods before me." (Exodus 20:1-3)

The most curious thing about the Ten Commandments is the way they begin. They do not start with a command at all. Before we are bombarded with a list of instructions, we have an introduction to the Instructor.

Some books leave this introductory piece out. Some commentators even suggest that it only crept in at a later stage when the law code had been set in its final shape. But I find that hard to accept. These first few words are far too crucial to ignore and much too fundamental to dismiss as an optional extra.

This brief sentence does, in fact, act as a powerful filter on a camera. It changes the way we see the picture made up by the commands and prohibitions that follow. It breathes life into a sterile code and adds warmth to its cold print. It launches the grim, earthbound business of obeying rules and regulations into the supernatural orbit of enjoying a love relationship with God.

Let's explore further.

INTRODUCING THE LAWGIVER

Personal law. Most of us take it for granted that law is something cold and impersonal. We are used to seeing our national lawmakers on the television screen, but that does not really make us feel very close to them as people. At the end of the day, we face the need to observe their rules with a feeling of resignation, if not of outright indignation. It's a case of *them* and *us*.

Right from the start, the Ten Commandments jolt us out of that frame of mind. As far as God and his law are concerned, it is a case of *I* and *you*, not them and us. The whole scene shifts from the impersonal to the personal. "I am the LORD *your* God," insists the Lawmaker.

There is a little touch in those words that

would have taken Moses' mind back to another dramatic occasion. The setting was similar. It must have seemed almost like an action replay.

A short time before, Moses had found himself standing on the slopes of the same mountain where God had now given him the Ten Commandments. Curious to find out why a bush was on fire but not reduced to ashes, he had gone to investigate. God had spoken to him from that fire, giving him his personal orders and promising rescue for the people of Israel from their slavery in Egypt. "Say to the Israelites: 'I AM has sent me to you'" (Exodus 3:14), he told Moses.

"I AM" was God's personal name, specially given to the Israelites to assure them that God was not impossibly remote, but constantly with them in an intimate relationship. The Hebrew letters form the word Yahweh, which most modern Bible versions translate "LORD" with capital letters.

So it is here. The great God who thundered his commandments from Mount Sinai was the personal LORD who had already kept his promise by rescuing his people from their life of slavery. These rules were not "barked at them by a capricious staff sergeant," as one writer puts it, but lovingly relayed by a God who was intimately concerned for his people's welfare. He was "I," not "it." And they were "you," not "them." The

Ten Commandments are not really a law code at
all. They are one side of a conversation between
friends.

Loving law. "Friendship," in fact, is far too
weak a word to describe the "I-you" relationship
between the Lord and his people. The Old Testament sometimes pictures it as a marriage.
"Return, faithless people," the Lord appealed,
when Israel had *committed adultery* by worshiping idols; "for I am your husband" (Jeremiah
3:14).

After thirty years of married life, the thought
that I can turn to my wife and say, "I am yours
and you are mine" still sends a tingle down my
spine. If there is a thrill in being able to share
that kind of intimacy with a fellow human
being, it nearly blows the mind to realize that
the almighty Creator of the universe thinks in
the same way about his people.

Yet this is the frame in which the Ten Commandments are set. When we pay attention as
"God speaks all these words," we are light years
away from a dry, clinical interview in a lawyer's
office or the tense, threatening atmosphere of a
police interview room. We are listening in to pil-
low talk.

There is one special aspect of God's love relationship with his people that is particularly

encouraging when we consider the Ten Commandments. The "grace factor" describes it best. The Bible uses the word *grace* to explain that unique kind of love that is freely given but totally undeserved.

The way the Bible describes the beginning of God's special relationship with his people illustrates the grace factor in his love very powerfully. It was no meeting of equals. The Old Testament is almost brutally blunt about that. "The LORD did not set his affection on you and choose you because you were more numerous than other peoples, for you were the fewest of all peoples," declares the book of Deuteronomy. "But it was because the LORD loved you" (7:7-8).

What was there in the Lord's chosen partner that prompted him to propose marriage? Absolutely nothing! She impressed nobody. He loved her simply and solely because he loved her. There was no other explanation, apart from amazing grace.

As we shall see, the fact that God takes the initiative in loving us makes an enormous difference in the way we respond to his commandments.

The grace factor made a vivid reappearance in Old Testament times whenever God's special relationship with his people hit the rocks. His total faithfulness to them was not always returned in kind—to put it very mildly. They abused his trust and insulted his love. They provoked his anger by going into public partnership with his enemies. In human terms, they provided him with every conceivable ground for a divorce. Total rejection was the least they deserved.

But God never rejected them. He lashed them through prophets' words and punished them through foreign powers, but he never wrote them off. Those were simply his devices to woo them back. The grace factor in his love, which made it so very special, responded to their needs, not to their merits.

Again, the fact that God's love is so constant and forgiving makes a huge difference in the way we react when he tells us to do things. The rebel son in Jesus' famous story must have responded in a completely different way to his father's instructions once he had been welcomed back with a love he knew he did not deserve.

Love in action. I once worked for a Christian student organization. Because I was out of the office a good deal, I was allowed the luxury of a secretary. While I visited colleges and universities, she had the much less exciting job of typing and mailing my letters.

As a matter of habit, I used to finish most of my letters by saying, "With my prayers." One day my secretary came to me looking worried. "Tell me honestly," she said, "do you *really* pray for all these people?" I think I blushed. I hope I did anyway. And I certainly changed my letter-writing habits. My promises of prayer were all words and no action.

Nowadays, I often end letters with the words "With my love in Christ." But the memory of my former secretary still haunts me. Do I really mean to show Christian love to those lucky people who receive my letters? Would I really respond practically if any of them needed my time or my money? Or am I all mouth? Perhaps "Yours sincerely" would be better. Or would it?

The New Testament encourages Christians to put their love into action. "Let us not love with words or tongue but with actions and in truth" (1 John 3:18).

God certainly did and does exactly that. In Old Testament times, he matched his expressions of warm love for his people with an act of rescue they could not ignore. The Ten Commandments begin by refreshing their memories. "I am the LORD your God, who brought you out of Egypt, out of the land of slavery." One week they were slaves, the next they were free. That was the measure of God's practical love.

Israel's prophets and songwriters never tired of reminding the people how powerfully active

God's love for them really was. "I am the LORD
your God, who brought you out of Egypt; . . ."
declares the Lord through Hosea. "I cared for
you in the desert, in the land of burning heat"
(Hosea 13:4-5). "I am the LORD your God, who
brought you up out of Egypt," echoes Psalm
81:10: "Open wide your mouth and I will fill it."

That great act of rescue from slavery in Egypt
was, of course, just the trailer for what was to
come. "God so loved the world that he gave his
one and only Son," said Jesus about himself
(John 3:16). "This is love," John comments,
"not that we loved God, but that he loved us and
sent his Son as an atoning sacrifice for our sins"
(1 John 4:10). The cross marked the climax of
God's love in action, when Jesus died to save us
from a fate far worse than slavery to any human
oppressor.

THE DEMANDS OF LOVE

Gratitude. Why begin a list of laws with a statement of love? In a word, *motivation!* When
someone does something especially generous
for you, it is only natural to look for some way
or other to express your gratitude to them.

Some time ago, a prison riot broke out. It
began in the chapel on a Sunday morning and
ended, weeks later, on the roof. In the meantime,

wardens and police were pelted daily with tiles and bricks and any other missiles the angry inmates could lay their hands on. At the inquiry that followed, a strange story unfolded. An inmate told how he had rescued a prison officer, his natural enemy, from possible death during the first hours of the rioting. The officer lay injured on the chapel floor, where he was being kicked senseless by an angry mob. At great risk to himself, the inmate had rescued the unconscious man and dragged him out of immediate danger.

At the inquiry, the injured officer publicly thanked his rescuer. He offered to stand up and speak for him in any court case that resulted. It was the least he could do for someone who had saved his life. He would have liked to do more.

This is the spirit in which the Ten Commandments are laid down. It is as though God is saying to his people, "I have done all this for you. I have picked you up from the floor. Remember Egypt? Now show how grateful you are by living for me in the following ten ways."

Before we move on, it is worth pausing to take in the unusual features of this biblical approach to rule keeping. Lawmakers usually back their demands by threats, not by appeals for gratitude.

The college in London where I work and live

has nearly sixty acres of lovely grounds. You can lose yourself with a book, if you want to, in the fields and woods. But there is one snag. Staff and student families own dogs, and Oak Hill dogs cause constant problems by fouling paths and lawns. One day, the college gardener's patience snapped. Beside one offending heap he left a notice that read, "The next one what does this will get shot." Those who got closer could read another sentence in smaller print underneath: "I mean the owner, not the dog."

That was an approach everyone understood. Canine behavior actually improved, until the notice got blown down. But I wonder what the attitude would have been if the gardener had written, "Look how nicely I keep this path. Show your gratitude by stopping your dog from fouling it."

All the Old Testament's laws are practical, detailed applications of the Ten Commandments. Some of them, certainly, are reinforced by threats. But far, far more often, people who are tempted to overstep the mark are brought back into line by reminders of God's generous love.

The law lays it down, for example, that slaves must be treated humanely. *Why?* "Remember that you were slaves in Egypt and the LORD your God redeemed you. That is why I give you this command today" (Deuteronomy 15:15). Busi-

ness people are told not to cheat. *Why not?*
Because their loving Lord did not cheat them
when they were especially vulnerable: "I am the
LORD your God, who brought you out of Egypt."
A stranger should always be treated generously.
Why? Again the answer is plain once the memo-
ries are jogged: "Love him as yourself, for you
were aliens in Egypt. I am the LORD your God"
(Leviticus 19:34).

So the Bible has its own special answer to all
the "Why should I?" questions that bubble up to
the surface when we are given orders: Remember God's amazing love—and show him how
grateful you are.

Faithfulness. The first commandment follows
as naturally as day follows night. "You shall
have no other gods before me." How could they,
when their loving Lord had liberated them so
dramatically from a life of slavery? And how
could *we* possibly do such a thing, when the
same Lord has freed us from the grip of sin and
introduced us to eternal living?

Very easily, of course! The Old Testament
believer was only too prone to forget all about
rescue from Egypt once his vineyard and olive
grove began to prosper in the Promised Land
(see Deuteronomy 6:10-12). And the modern
prosperous Christian knows how simple it is to

surrender mastery of his life—even unintention-
ally—to the great god Money (see Matthew
6:24).

That is no doubt why this commandment has
a negative ring about it. We need a strong fence
to stop us from straying from the exclusive commitment that God requires of us.

Positively, this total dedication is summed up
in another of the Old Testament's laws that Jesus
highlighted: "The LORD our God, the LORD is
one. Love the LORD your God with all your heart
and with all your soul and with all your
strength" (Deuteronomy 6:4-5; see also Matthew 22:37). Such total devotion leaves no room
for other claimants.

The parallel with marriage is obvious. God
loves his people as a husband loves his wife.
And he looks for the same faithful attachment in
return. Bachelor days are gone, as far as the
believer is concerned. Flirting with rivals to the
Lord's marital rights is most definitely out.

The quality of this central relationship is crucial. If it is right, there will be no problems in
coping with the demands of the other nine commandments. Even if we do not understand or
appreciate some of them, our loving commitment to our loving Lord will make obedience
easier. If my wife told me, "I've got a surprise
for you. Shut your eyes and hold your hand out,"

I would do it. If anyone else made the same request, I would make sure I peeked first. It is all a matter of trust.

Jesus made the same point by contrasting friends and servants. "You are my *friends* if you do what I command," he told his disciples. "I no longer call you *servants*" (John 15:14-15, emphasis mine).

Both friends and slaves are called to obey, but they do so for quite different reasons. The slave conforms because he has to; the friend because he wants to. The slave finds obedience a drag, a heavy burden to bear. But the friend who enjoys a close relationship with the master honestly wants to do the master's will. The burden is lifted. John puts it in a nutshell: "This is love for God: to obey his commands. And his commands are not burdensome" (1 John 5:3).

All this helps us to understand how the Bible can describe keeping God's law as exciting. Listen to these words from Psalm 119, for example. "Direct me in the path of your commands, for there I find delight. Turn my heart toward your statutes and not towards selfish gain. . . . The law from your mouth is more precious to me than thousands of pieces of silver and gold" (verses 35-36, 72).

If that expression of devotion to the law does not strike us as going right over the top, it may help to translate it into more familiar law-keeping language. "Direct me in the path of the income tax legislation," we might begin, "for there I find delight. Turn my heart toward the small print and not toward selfish gain. The rulings from the inspector's computer are more precious to me than thousands of pieces of silver and gold."

The reason this sounds so ludicrous has to do with relationships. The tax collector does not love me. I would feel embarrassed if I thought he or she did. If I were to break the tax regulations, it would not occur to me that I had personally wounded the faceless somebody who sends me all those complicated forms. There is no close relationship between the two of us to be strained or broken.

Wholeness. Scholars are not completely certain what the expression "before me" in the first commandment implies. The two Hebrew words literally mean "before my face." The whole commandment can be understood either as a veto on having *additional* deities or as a warning against allowing other deities *supremacy* over the Lord.

The answer probably lies in a combination of both ideas. The Old Testament insists, of course, that only one God exists. All other so-called deities are shams. But, once they were settled in Canaan, the people of Israel rubbed shoulders with men and women from an alien culture who accepted polytheism all too readily. Deities of both sexes and with different roles were to be found around every corner. And God's people were sorely tempted not only to believe in these "other gods" but to give them priority over their one and only Lord.

The polytheist dealt with a whole crowd of deities. There was a god for every department of life; one for work, another for home, yet another who looked after the crops, and even one to hear your agonized prayers when you got a toothache.

As a result, life was lived in a series of separate compartments. Each deity demanded different standards of behavior within his or her special sector. With care, one god could be played off another to serve the worshiper's own selfish ends. The husband who got drunk and smashed up his home might have offended the family deities, but he could at least plead in mitigation that the god of wine had been at the top of his list for worship that day.

That sounds absurd, but it is not a million miles away from the life-style many of us live today. Some modern people are really old-time polytheists in thin disguise. They divide their lives into separate compartments and apply different moral standards to each. A politician will make promises he knows he cannot keep in an election address, but would never dream of going back on his word to a friend. A business-man will tell his secretary to keep all visitors at bay by saying he is out, but would get very angry indeed if it was ever suggested that he might tell a lie to his wife.

Ancient or modern, such divided behavior is on a collision course with the Bible's "one God" approach to life. That is certainly the implication of the first commandment. The Old Testament believer was bound in obedience to one Lord who governed everything he did. Whether he was doing something religious (like making a sacrifice) or something political (like settling a dispute) or something businesslike (like lending money), he did it all before the Lord's face. The same set of God-given standards applied to every department of life.

This is why the Ten Commandments cover such a huge span of human experience. The first four are more religious than moral and the last six are more moral than religious, but there is no way some can be kept and the rest thrown out. Any appeal to have moral standards without reli-gion, or to engage in a spirituality that has noth-ing to do with politics or economics, capsizes on the "one God" rock. The whole of life is all one God-centered piece.

So the first commandment sets the tone for all the rest. It points us to a God whose practical, saving love makes obedience a delight; and whose all-embracing claims rescue us from becoming schizophrenic one-person civil wars. That is surely a more inspiring, exciting curtain-raiser than any other law code can boast.

TO THINK AND TALK ABOUT

1. "I am the LORD your God. . . ." Why is he your God (see Deuteronomy 7:7-8)? What is your reaction to what the author calls the "grace factor"?

2. The Lord has shown his love for you by bring-ing you out of the slavery of sin. How can you show your gratitude?

3. How do your answers to questions 1 and 2 affect your view of the Ten Commandments and your motivation to obey them?

4. "You shall have no other gods before me." What does this mean? Why do you think God put this commandment at the head of the list?

5. What else do you find yourself putting before God? In view of his great love for you and the

way he has delivered you, why do you think you are still tempted to do this?

6. How do you think you could keep prompting yourself to put God first in all aspects of your everyday life?

FOUR
A God without Rivals: The Second Commandment

You shall not make for yourself an idol in the form of anything in heaven above or on the earth beneath or in the waters below. You shall not bow down to them or worship them; for I, the LORD your God, am a jealous God, punishing the children for the sin of the fathers to the third and fourth generation of those who hate me, but showing love to a thousand generations of those who love me and keep my commandments. (Exodus 20:4-6)

In the way it is presented, the second commandment is a mirror image of the first. The first began with a statement about God and finished with a word of command. The second starts with a command and ends by telling us more about God.

The themes are similar, too. But while the main thrust of the first commandment is a call to commitment, the second commandment deals in greater detail with those "idols" or "other gods" that compete with the Lord for the high ground of our lives. And while the first paints a vivid picture of God's love in action, the second draws an equally striking but much more somber portrait of God as Judge.

WHAT IS AN IDOL?

At the front of my home church there are two visual aids for worshipers. Fixed to the wall are sturdy, stone slabs with the words of the Ten Commandments engraved on them. And between them is a head-and-shoulders portrait of Jesus. Are those things idols, within the meaning of the second commandment? If so, I should be petitioning the church council to have them thrown out.

In our college chapel, we have a very fine colored tapestry. It is rich in symbolism, featuring a cross, a dove, a crown, and a bowl of water (to remind ministers-to-be that Jesus washed his disciples' feet). The side walls of the chapel are often bright with banners. Most have words of Scripture stitched on them, illustrated very imaginatively with scenes of various kinds in the background. It is enough to make a Puritan's blood boil. Should mine be boiling, too?

It is not really enough to reply that these things cannot possibly be idols because no one physically bows down to them. Idolatry is misdirected worship, and worship is an attitude of mind and heart. An idol is anything that attracts the heartfelt devotion that properly belongs to the Lord alone. Perhaps I will only know if there are people in my church who actually worship that picture of Jesus when I measure their reactions if it is ever taken down.

Centuries ago, Augustine wrote some very wise words about idolatry that build a sturdy bridge between Old Testament times and our own. This is what he said:

> Idolatry is worshiping anything that ought to be used, or using anything that ought to be worshiped.

That is worth a closer look.

WORSHIPING CREATION

In his letter to the Romans, Paul condemns those who "worshiped and served created things rather than the Creator." People who do that kind of thing, he comments, have "exchanged the truth of God for a lie" (Romans 1:25). In other words, putting anything at the controls of your life, where God alone should be, is standing life on its head. It is like putting the luggage in the pilot's seat, pretending that it has the know-how to fly the plane. It is living a lie. Created things are meant to be used, not worshiped. That is the truth of the matter in God's world. Reversing the roles is dangerous, as well as stupid.

Those who are attracted to the modern environmental protection movement should take careful note of that. Conservationists have a great deal of God's truth on their side. But when their keenness to preserve the world's resources makes them unwilling to put any of them to human use, they are only one short step away from idolatry.

Years ago now, I met a group of young men wandering through our college grounds. We got talking, and they were very interested to discover that they had strayed into a theological college. We discussed what we believed.

They belonged to a commune that was passionately committed to the promotion of green values. "Do you see that tree?" one of them asked me. "We believe a tree is every bit as valuable as a human being. Do you believe that?"

I had to confess that I did not. My Christian faith told me that trees should be respected, because God made them. Rain forests should not be demolished to pander to shortsighted human greed. But trees are God-made, not God-like. And they are made to be used. To think otherwise is to push the pendulum much too far in the direction of pantheism, which grants divine status to everything. And that is idolatry.

People can make idols out of anything, of course. That is why the wording of this commandment is so broad. Sportsmen can make a god out of a putter or a pair of spikes. Housewives can turn a roomful of furniture into a holy of holies that can only be entered when you have taken your shoes off. Students may idolize the prospect of a first-class degree. There is no end to the idol-making business.

The Bible puts its finger on three of life's created features that men and women have put on pedestals and worshiped from that time to this. All three become the focal points of later commandments, so we shall meet them again later. J. I. Packer sums them up very neatly as "sex, shekel, and stomach."

Sex, shekel, and stomach. Most of us do not need a session on the psychiatrist's couch to persuade us how easily the drives for sexual satisfaction, food, and drink can dominate us. And people who say that the things money can buy really mean nothing to them are usually the first to ask for a loan. I shall never forget a charming neighbor who was totally dedicated to the simple life but who was always coming around to borrow my lawn mower.

The Bible warns us very clearly about the subtle takeover bids sex, money, and food make for the center spot in our lives. And each can threaten us from completely different angles.

Promiscuity can turn *sex* into an idol, carefully massaged by late-night films on TV and by the advertising business. In his first letter to the Christians at Corinth, a city famous for its red-light district, Paul reminds Christians that their bodies are temples where the Holy Spirit lives. They are parts of the body of Christ. Sex must never be worshiped in God's temple. To his critics who protested, "Ah yes, but Christ has set us free from all those petty inhibitions," Paul replies, "I am allowed to do anything, but I am not going to let anything make me its slave" (1 Corinthians 6:12, TEV).

"Keep sex at arm's length, and it will never dominate you." Is that what Paul means here? Not quite! Saying a loud no to sex does not guarantee that you will always be free from its grip. In the very next chapter, Paul exposes the idolatry of sex *avoidance*. There were Christians at Corinth (sickened, perhaps, by their past habits) who were saying, "It is good for a man not to marry" (1 Corinthians 7:1). That, too, was wrong (verse 9). These Christians were showing that sex still tyrannized them by the frightened way they campaigned against it. Even a crusade against sexual permissiveness can be every bit as idolatrous as the most blatant promiscuity if it fills all of life's horizons.

So sex can preoccupy us in opposite ways. And when it does, it takes a place in our lives that belongs to God alone.

Money, too, can make a double-pronged assault on God's place of supremacy in any person's life. In Luke 12, Jesus tells his story about the rich fool who made an idol out of his wealth. But the Lord then went straight on to reproach those whose *lack* of cash dominated their lives by making them worry perpetually where their next meal was coming from (verses 22-31).

I think of a young couple I married. Their wedding service came from the old Anglican prayer book. When we got to the part where he had to say to her, "And with all my worldly goods I thee endow," I could see them both shaking with laughter. He didn't have a bean, and she knew it. He was going into the church's ministry, so their financial prospects were fairly bleak.

On their wedding day, it did not matter at all. But many ministries have been blighted by money worries later, when the children need new shoes and when big heating bills drop through the mailbox. It is tough teaching for the badly off, but Jesus' stern warning, "You cannot serve both God and Money" (Matthew 6:24), applies just as much to the "have-nots" as it does to the "haves." Idolatry is a sword that has two edges.

The Bible's teaching about *food and drink* takes a similar line. There are those whose "god is their stomach" (Philippians 3:19). And there are those who deliberately abstain from certain food and drink, looking down their noses at people who do not share their convictions (Romans 14:3). Both sets of people are idolaters, because both are preoccupied with their diets. They both need to take Paul's advice, "Whether you eat or drink or whatever you do, do it all for the glory of God" (1 Corinthians 10:31).

Nowhere does the Bible say that sex, money, food, or drink are bad things in themselves. As Paul himself points out to Timothy, it is hypocritical heretics who "forbid people to marry and order them to abstain from certain foods, which God created to be received with thanksgiving by those who believe and who know the truth. For everything God created is good, and nothing is to be rejected if it is received with thanksgiving" (1 Timothy 4:3-4).

All these things are great—in their place. But God provides them to be used, not to be worshiped. They become idols at the moment when they are treated as ends instead of means.

People, too. It is not only things that threaten to unseat God from his position of supremacy. People can become idols, too.

As usual, the Greeks had a word for it. As well as several other expressions for "love," they used the word *storgé* to describe that special kind of bond that ties families tightly together.

There is nothing wrong with *storgé,* of course. The Bible strongly encourages husbands to love their wives ("just as Christ loved the church and gave himself up for her," writes Paul—Ephesians 5:25). And a grown-up child who feels no special responsibility for his or her aging parents "has denied the faith and is worse than an unbeliever" (1 Timothy 5:8).

Nevertheless, there is a world of difference between generous love and blindfolded bias.

Storgé becomes idolatry when a couple see marriage as an in-growing alliance to defy the rest of the world. The triple locks on the door and the high garden fences all convey the same message: Keep out! And children become idols when their parents fight tooth and nail to get them into the best schools, without a care in the world about the education other people's kids get.

That is not genuine family love, as the Bible teaches it. It is corporate selfishness. And it lurks behind all kinds of other ugly behavior when groups of people band together.

As I write this, the media have gone football crazy. The World Cup is in full swing. There are two or three hours of soccer on television every day. But as well as competition on the field (some of it healthy), the press is busy reporting fights between rival fans outside the stadiums. That is the point where support becomes idolatry. No one minds a football team having a supporters' club. But most people object when support *for* a team degenerates into all-out war *against* other teams and their fans. Only idols need to be protected by hostile prejudice.

And me! Stafford Clark, the psychologist, has wisely written, "No one is born prejudiced against other people, but everyone is born prejudiced in favor of himself." There he has penetrated right to the heart of "person idolatry." Because I am a sinner, the person I am most likely to idolize is myself.

We dress up self-worship today in respectable clothing. It hides its hideous face behind perfectly legitimate masks such as the search for self-fulfillment or the personal need for self-actualization. But when these fashionable terms hide the idolizing of self, God longs to rip away the disguise and expose the oldest rival there is to his mastery of our lives.

Even a move into some branch of Christian service can be an ego trip in disguise.

I have seen several generations of students pass through their training here at Oak Hill and become ordained ministers in the church. Most of them come back later, either for a reunion or just because they want to revisit their old haunts. My stock conversation-opener when I met an Old Oak (as we call them) used to be, "Well, are you enjoying your ministry?" To which the stock answer was something like, "Yes, it's fantastic. It's great fun."

Behind the confident smiles, I sometimes noticed hurt eyes. No, the ministry is not always much fun. Serving God does not always massage the ego with a succession of spiritual thrills. To go into it with that self-centered expectation is really a surrender to idolatry.

So I have stopped asking my stupid question in case I get any more hypocritical answers. Whether we wear our collars back-to-front or not, why should we expect to *enjoy* our Christian service? If we are in the places God wants us to be, we ought to find life fulfilling, but there is a world of difference between the satisfaction of knowing that you are pleasing Christ and the amusement of an ego trip.

Jesus did not always enjoy his ministry. He got tired and he went hungry. Other people misunderstood him, sometimes deliberately. He shed tears over a dead friend and a faithless city. Life, for him, ended in the early thirties in hideous physical, mental, and spiritual pain. No, it was not much fun.

But that was not the point, was it? Jesus did not come into the world to enjoy himself. He was not on a glorified ego trip. As he put it himself, "the Son of Man did not come to be served, but to serve, and to give his life as a ransom for many" (Mark 10:45). For him, as for us, the antidote to idolatry was self-giving service.

There is, of course, a healthy kind of self-esteem. If I know that God loves me, I must not despise what he values. And the Bible tells me that I bear his image. My Maker surely cannot want me to hate the self that bears his likeness.

Nevertheless, wholesome self-esteem can too easily slip into sick self-worship. It was to protect his followers against that deadly form of idolatry—and its extension, ingrown *storgé*—that Jesus delivered some of his sternest warnings. "If anyone would come after me, he must

deny himself and take up his cross and follow
me" (Mark 8:34). "Anyone who loves his father
or mother more than me is not worthy of me;
anyone who loves his son or daughter more than
me is not worthy of me" (Matthew 10:37).

USING THE CREATOR

The Bible is very stern in its condemnations of
idolatry. But it is also very humorous. The Old
Testament prophets are particularly biting in the
way they ridicule idol-worshipers. "How incredi-
bly stupid to construct a god out of something
you have made," mocks Isaiah, "even if you are
a self-made man." "Want to know what your
'gods' remind me of?" echoes Jeremiah. "A
scarecrow in a melon patch!" (see Isaiah 44:12-
17 and Jeremiah 10:3-5).

Modern idols are just as ridiculous, when you
think about it. A Christian who idolizes a God-
substitute, when he or she has direct access to
God himself through Jesus, is like a lover who
prefers a photograph to the loved one.

I once had a friend who was separated from
his fiancée for months at a time. She gave him a
small china rabbit that winked, as a reminder of
her. That rabbit occupied pride of place among
John's possessions during their times of separa-
tion. But I can imagine what her reaction would

have been if he had insisted on cuddling the rabbit when she arrived on the scene herself.

Why, then, do people worship God-substitutes? Why do *we* do it?

Augustine had the answer. Remember, he said that as well as "worshiping anything that ought to be used," idolatry is "using anything that ought to be worshiped."

For *anything,* read *someone.* Idolatry's great fascination lies in its misleading guarantee. It offers its worshipers the capacity to use God and to tap his power. It cannot deliver the goods, of course, but there are at least three different ways in which we can fall for the bogus promise.

God on a leash. The Bible insists that the devil is real. He is an astute, powerful enemy who must be taken seriously. So what do people do? They caricature him by giving him horns, a forked tail, and a stupid leer. Then they tie him to a piece of elastic, dangle him as an ornament in their cars, and ask in triumph, Who can possibly be frightened by such a ridiculous figment of the human imagination?

Alternatively, they dabble in the occult. They toy with horoscopes and play with Ouija boards, trying to tap this mysterious power they only half believe in. They do it either to satisfy their curiosity about "the other side" or to be reunited with dead relations. If spiritual powers exist, they are there to be used, rather like a mysterious kind of electricity.

Some people treat God in much the same way. If they do not want to believe in him, they invent a caricature. God is a benevolent old man who lives on a cloud. He is totally out of touch with the realities of a nuclear age, but he is a valuable part of the culture, and children should know about him. He is there to be used, especially at Christmas time and for nice weddings in church. But to worship him would be embarrassing. It might turn you into a religious fanatic.

Christians, of course, believe with all their hearts that God is real. We have experienced his power in our own lives, and we earnestly pray that others will know his power in theirs. But even Christians are prone to use God, instead of worship him. We are perplexed if we tap the divine power at an all-night prayer meeting and the answers we confidently expect are not there in the morning. We lay hands on two sick people and cannot understand why one gets better and the other does not.

A young Christian couple I know are longing for a baby. Doctors have told them that there is no medical reason why they should not become parents. They and their friends have prayed regularly and resolutely for the happy event, but years have passed now and the wife is still not pregnant. After going through a particularly bad time, her husband told me, "We know we must let God be God."

That reaction to frustration deeply impressed me. It is the perfect antidote to idolatry. The explosive power of the living God cannot be harnessed. He is never at our disposal. We cannot bargain with him. He is there to be worshiped, not manipulated.

God in a group. I once worked for three years in a town where three churches of different denominations competed for congregations within a few hundred yards of one another. I am sure I was not the only one to wonder why they did not all get together and share a single building, if only to reduce the repair and heating bills.

Many people have asked similar questions about the existence of different religions. Why have synagogues, mosques, temples, and churches within a stone's throw, when worshipers from all religions could get together under one roof? We might even learn more about the Supreme Deity—and throw fewer stones—if we set out to learn from each other's spiritual traditions.

That seemed a sensible thing to do in Old Testament times, too. The Lord had rescued Israel from Egypt. As the God of the nation, he must obviously be worshiped. But once the people had settled in Canaan, they found themselves in a multifaith culture. There were strange gods in this fertile land whose specialty was to make every harvest a success. So why not worship them as well? Pooling the combined resources of all the deities around might well enrich everyone's experience of the divine—and raise the standard of living.

Ancient or modern, this is a sophisticated form of idolatry. It breathes the air of tolerance. But it is idolatry nevertheless. It treats religion like an insurance policy. The more coverage you can get the better, so if other deities offer different options, go for a portfolio!

The God of the Bible refuses to be used like that. He claims to be unique. All other so-called gods are false. To worship them alongside him is idolatrous. He demands his worshipers' exclusive devotion.

God in my image. At the beginning of this chapter, I mentioned a portrait of Jesus that hangs in my local church. Some people find that picture a helpful aid to worship because it accurately represents the way they see Jesus. Others think of Jesus quite differently, so they find it more of a hindrance than a help.

We all picture God in different ways. That is inevitable. But some of us go farther and insist that the way *we* see him is the only right way. We construct a mental image of God and worship that.

This is inward idolatry. And it poses a double threat to our spiritual health. In the first place, it means that our image of God is likely to be false because it is partial. The New Testament tells us, for example, to "consider therefore the kindness *and* sternness of God" (Romans 11:22, emphasis mine). We may find it very hard to hold those two aspects of God's character together in our mind's eye. So the temptation is to construct a one-sided image of God. We see him as a kind uncle who smiles benignly on everything we do, or as a stern, grim judge who frightens us in nightmares.

Secondly, we are liable to reject the features of God's character that we do not like. This is why so many of the Jewish leaders rejected Jesus. He claimed to be God, but he did not measure up to the image of God they had already constructed in their own minds. The only two possible conclusions were that they were wrong (which was unthinkable) or that his claim was false. So, in John's words, "He was in the world, and though the world was made through him, the world did not recognize him" (John 1:10).

We are really back to self-worship. If we insist that God can only be as we want him to be, we have effectively tried to create him in our own image. And that is idolatry. "It were better to have no opinion of God at all," commented Francis Bacon, "than such an opinion as is unworthy of him."

GOD'S JEALOUSY

Idolatry is serious. No one who reads the second commandment all the way through to the end can be in any doubt about that. The warnings attached to breaking this instruction of God's are fearsomely frank.

Where we see cause and effect, the Bible often describes God in action. So it is here. He will punish idolatrous practice, we are told, "to the third and fourth generation."

It is not nearly so hard as we sometimes make out to see this "reap what you sow" principle in operation. The idolizing of sex in Western society a decade ago, for example, has left obvious disasters in its wake today.

Promiscuity has raised the divorce rate and spread the AIDS virus. Not every individual who contracts AIDS or gets a divorce is being directly punished by God, of course, for his or her personal sin. It is vital to stress that. Nor is sex always the culprit when a marriage breaks down or an HIV test proves positive. But the fact remains that these social and physical diseases spread fastest when attitudes to intercourse outside marriage are most permissive. And behind that state of affairs Christians recognize the results of disobedience to God's law by the community as a whole.

The evidence is plain for all who are willing to see it. Sex makes a wonderful servant but a terrible master. And the effects of disobedience travel down through the generations. Children are inevitably affected, and their children will be, too.

In a morally ordered universe, a society that flouts God's laws must expect to reap what it sows. But that is not all. God also rewards with lasting love the community that demonstrates its devotion to him by obeying his commands. As if to highlight the bounty of his love, and to put his judgment in its right perspective, the commandment expresses their ratio as a thousand to four. Judgment is God's "strange work" (Isaiah 28:21). He is "slow to anger," but "abounding in love" (Psalm 103:8).

Indeed, it is God's love that makes him so jealous. To us, jealousy is an ugly characteristic. But in God's case it is the pure expression of his righteous anger when a rival threatens to lure his people from his loving care.

In one of his books, David Cook tells how he felt when an English male guest greeted his wife by kissing her. As a good Scot, his first instinct was to smash his visitor in the face. Only later did he discover that a kiss on the cheek is an acceptable greeting south of the border.

If that Englishman had found himself sitting unexpectedly on his host's doormat with a bleeding nose, he might have appreciated (later, perhaps!) that jealousy can be an expression of outraged love. In the second commandment, God is pictured as a furious husband who has come home to find his wife being raped. The root of the Hebrew word for "jealous" means "red." God is red with righteous anger, not green with envy, when he confronts his rivals. His burning love does not allow him to tolerate any competition for his people's affections.

This has been a long chapter, but the theme is an important one. Idolatry is insidious. It turns the proper relationship of creature to Creator upside down by inviting us to worship what we should use and to use the one whom we should worship. Even the trappings of our church services (sound systems and song books, as well as crucifixes and communion wafers) can become idols if we make them ends instead of means.

In Old Testament times, with very few exceptions, God chose to reveal himself by words, not by visual appearances. That was to stop his people copying what they glimpsed and worshiping the false, partial images they produced. "You saw no form of any kind the day the LORD spoke to you," God reminded them. "Therefore watch yourselves very carefully, so that you do not become corrupt and make for yourselves an idol, an image of any shape" (Deuteronomy 4:15-16).

Then, at the first Christmas, God's Word became flesh and blood. At last, God's people were able to see him and touch him for themselves (1 John 1:1). Jesus is "the image of the invisible God," wrote Paul (Colossians 1:15). "Anyone who has seen me," Jesus told one of his followers, "has seen the Father" (John 14:9).

Before Jesus arrived, God spoke *through* his prophets. After Jesus came, he spoke—and still speaks—*in* his Son. We may worship Jesus, because in him God is accurately and uniquely unveiled. But to worship anyone or anything else is idolatry.

TO THINK AND TALK ABOUT

1. What is an idol?

2. What are your idols? If you can, share your temptations in your group so that you can support one another in the struggle against them.

3. How can you love someone without idolizing them?

4. Do you agree that our biggest idol is self? What is the difference between a healthy self-esteem and self-idolatry?

5. The author says that one form of idolatry is to use God instead of worshiping him. How might even Christians fall into this trap? Do you recognize this tendency in yourself?

6. The second commandment speaks of "punishing the children for the sin of the fathers. . . ." How does the author explain this difficult warning? Do you agree with him?

7. In the previous chapter we considered God's love. Now we are told that he is a "jealous" God. How can he be both loving and jealous?

FIVE
Take Care with Your Intimacies: The Third Commandment

> *You shall not misuse the name of the LORD your God, for the LORD will not hold anyone guiltless who misuses his name. (Exodus 20:7)*

Names are important. If people remember your name, it shows they care. And if they forget who you are, especially when you expect them to remember, it can hurt.

One summer Sunday, I was standing in the vestry of a small country church. The minister was away. I was going to take the evening service, but first I was introduced to the choir.

There was just one of her. We stood there a little awkwardly. "What do you do?" I asked, in a clumsy attempt to get the conversation going.

"I keep pigs," she replied.

"And how many pigs do you have?" This was not going to be easy!

She did not have to stop to think. "A hundred and ninety-two at the moment."

"Really?" I laughed. "Are you certain of that? Are you sure there aren't two hundred?"

"Of course I'm sure," she said, bristling with indignation. "I've got names for them all, haven't I?"

There was no answer to that. The idea of knowing l92 pigs by name had me beaten. I thought guiltily how long it had taken my wife and me to work out names for our third child. But when I got home and pondered on that brief conversation, I realized how lucky those pigs were. They had a herdswoman who bothered enough to give them all names. She was not just into pigs for the money. She really cared.

The good shepherd, said Jesus, "calls his own sheep by name" (John 10:3). No wonder they follow *him!* Jesus was, of course, talking about his relationship with his human followers. "The measure of my love," he was telling them, "is that I can put a name to each one of you."

That is a mind-blowing thought. The Master of the universe can pick me out of a crowd as surely as he called Zacchaeus down from his tree. He knows who I am. And he never forgets my name. That is hard to credit.

But there is something even more amazing than that, according to the Bible. As well as calling me by name, God invites me to call him by his.

CALLING GOD BY HIS NAME

That was something the Jews found almost impossible to accept. They felt rather as I did when my vicar first asked me to call him Fred. I can do it now, but it seemed all wrong then. He was so much older, wiser, and more distinguished than I. So for three years I improvised by calling him nothing at all.

The Jews did something like that. They did all they could to avoid using the name of God altogether. And when a scribe was copying a manuscript and reached the four consonants that stood for Yahweh, the LORD's name, he had to observe a set of strict regulations. First he washed, then he put on full dress uniform, and finally he made sure he had ink on his quill so that he did not have to dip it in the pot half way through. And any visitor who interrupted him while he was writing—even the king—had to be ignored.

God never revealed himself by an image in Old Testament times. But each of his names was a self-revelation opening the curtains of eternity just a chink to allow us to glimpse vital aspects of his character.

The Hebrew words usually translated "God" (variants of *El*) express his power, his eternity and his all-seeing wisdom (see Genesis 16:13; 21:33; Exodus 6:3). *Adonai,* which comes across as "Lord" in our English versions, conveys his all-embracing rule (see Deuteronomy 10:17). And *Yahweh,* his personal name for himself, assures his people of his constant love, his awesome sternness, and his endless patience (see Exodus 34:6-7).

Jesus asked his disciples to address God as "Father" (Matthew 6:9). That highlighted another dimension of the divine nature. And Jesus' own name declares God's love in its most stupendous expression of all. "You are to give him the name Jesus," the angel instructed Joseph, "because he will save his people from their sins" (Matthew 1:21).

When we hear two people dropping the formalities and calling one another by their personal names, we assume they are on friendly terms with each other. That is the background against which we should read the third of the Ten Commandments. God wants us to enjoy a close relationship with him. Because he loves us, he knows our names. And he does not want that expression of intimacy to be one-sided. He asks us to use—but not to misuse—his own names in return.

The word *misuse* sounds the warning note, of course. And we badly need to hear it. By inviting us to be on personal-name terms with him, God has made himself vulnerable to abuse.

More than twenty years ago, when I was a junior member of staff, my principal overheard a student calling me by my first name. He took me to one side. "You should never allow that," he advised me. "Some students will never respect you if you let them call you David."

I think he was wrong. It happens all the time now. But I know what he meant. When we open the door of our lives to any kind of intimacy, we take a risk. The privilege may be abused. It is safer to keep people at arms' length than let them get close to you.

So it is in our relationship with God. He invites us to use his name. When we call him, he will listen and respond. It is an amazing privilege. How might we abuse it?

ENJOYING HIS INTIMACY
Being on personal-name terms with God gives us immense freedom and joy when we worship him. We can "praise his name" as we "proclaim his salvation" and "enter his gates with thanksgiving" (Psalms 96:2; 100:4). And, as Christians, we have the enormous privilege of unrestricted access to his presence. "For where

two or three come together in my name," promised Jesus, "there am I with them" (Matthew 18:20).

I am an Anglican, and we Anglicans are sometimes (though not always!) rather stuffy in our worship. Our service books can stifle spontaneity, if we use them too woodenly, and our set prayers can make our conversations with God a little stilted and formal.

In my teens I began attending a church where formality was considered a virtue. One or two of us rebelled and started a small prayer group. We used the church hall each week and sat around in a circle, praying informally. The vicar was far from pleased when he found out. "The proper way to pray to almighty God," he told us, "is in church on your knees."

We were right and he was right—though we could not see much merit in *his* case at the time. God surely wants us to worship him without inhibition. He does not mind us sitting down (or standing up) to pray. In the intimacy of prayer, the words that come most naturally to us are the ones he most wants to hear, even if the grammar would not always satisfy an English language examiner. And there is a valid place for emotion—for dancing and for tears—in expressing our heartfelt joy and our penitence in his presence.

Yes, but there is a place for reverence and awe as well, when we approach almighty God. That was the vicar's point. An invitation to meet God at close quarters should make us tremble, as well as shout for joy. In Bible times, you did not expect to survive the experience if you were "privileged" to meet God face-to-face (see, for example, Judges 13:19-22). And the natural reaction when his majestic holiness exposed your sinfulness at close quarters was to run away, not to get nearer to him (see Isaiah 6:5 and Luke 5:8).

God wants us to worship him in the intimacy of close fellowship. That is good and right. But to shamble carelessly into his presence with our spiritual hands in our pockets is an abuse of that privilege. It is an insulting misuse of his name.

When we think of insulting God, our minds probably go first to the abuse of his name as a swearword. That is certainly a practice that the third commandment bans. But blasphemy is usually a symptom of distance from God, not an abuse of intimacy.

When I was a student, I used to work for the local government during my vacations, doing manual jobs in parks and open spaces. It was not long before someone asked me what I was training to do, and the awful secret came out. I was going to be a vicar. Apart from the predictable jokes, this incredible piece of news had one

other fascinating result. Without me saying anything at all, the language changed. For one
whole summer, the accepted swearword in our
little crew was "Sorry, David."

It was only one of the jokes, of course. But it
was also an opportunity. It gave me the chance
to explain that—while I disliked the usual
stream of *F*s and *B*s anyway—the thing I found
it hardest to take was the careless use of "God!"
"Christ!" and "Jee-sus!" To them these words
were nothing more than a set of punctuation
marks, but to me the way they were used was an
insult to someone I knew and loved. I would
have felt much the same if they had insulted my
wife. Most of them understood what I meant.
And one day the foreman asked me into his hut
to tell him how he, too, could get to know God
in this intimate way.

Unbelief can lead to the misuse of God's
name, but so can belief. *Over*familiarity with
God erodes reverence, and that is an abuse that
is as hateful to him as any expletive.

LIVING IN HIS PRESENCE
In Old Testament times, people used God's
name to convince others that they were being
honest. Human nature being what it is, the temptation to be economical with the truth was as
powerful then as it is now, especially if there

were no witnesses around to expose a lie. So God was brought in as a kind of third party, the invisible witness to everything. Because nothing escaped his notice, you would not dare to call on his name to support an untruth. At least, that was the theory.

Suppose, says the Old Testament law (Exodus 22:10-11), that you ask a neighbor to look after one of your animals while you are away. When you get back, you find him acutely embarrassed. Your animal has apparently disappeared. How do you know he has not sold it himself and pocketed the cash? No one saw the thief. Well, said the law, your neighbor must take an oath before the Lord that he is being honest with you. If he does that, you just have to accept his word for it and put up with the loss.

"Do not swear falsely by my name and so profane the name of your God," the Lord warned his people (Leviticus 19:12). And, by and large, God's people did not misuse his name in that way. The prospect of his judgment, backed by capital punishment if they were ever found out, made a very effective deterrent.

What they actually did was something worse. They built an ingenious bypass around this God-given guarantee of honesty.

Instead of swearing by God's name, it became common practice to take oaths by some object associated with him (such as the temple, or an altar). Such vows could be worded very piously and impressively, so that simple people who did not read the small print were completely taken in. An oath not taken *specifically* in God's name, claimed the ecclesiastical solicitors, was not worth the parchment it was written on.

Jesus exposed that hypocritical hairsplitting with his usual bluntness. The whole object of calling God as your witness, he told his disciples, is to protect the truth, not to evade it. Using weasel words to justify a lie in God's name is an outrageous breach of the third commandment. Christians should not be in the business of building bypasses around the truth at all. They should be men and women of their word (Matthew 5:33-37).

Did Jesus mean that Christians should never take an oath in God's name in a law court? Some believe that he did. I knew an army chaplain once who appeared before the local magistrates on a driving charge. It was his word against a policeman's. He pleaded not guilty but refused to take the oath in the witness box, explaining that his conscience would not allow him to use God's name in that way. The magistrates took the view—unfairly, I thought—that he must be guilty if, as a man wearing a clergy collar, he was unwilling to summon God as his witness.

Jesus probably did not intend to ban oath taking altogether. When the high priest put him on oath "by the living God" to say whether or not he was the Christ, he did not object (Matthew 26:63-64). What Jesus did condemn was the practice of using religious language to conceal dishonesty. God sees through that kind of feeble human smoke screen.

The ninth commandment will have more to teach us about truthfulness. But in the meantime the third commandment leaves us in no doubt that people who whitewash their lies by calling on God as a witness are misusing his name in a particularly repulsive way.

USING HIS POWER

There was a widespread belief in ancient times that knowing people's names gave you power over them. And if that was true of ordinary men and women, it had to be even more true of God. If you could only discover God's real name, it was thought, you would have a handle on the most powerful force in the universe.

The Bible often associates God's name with power. One of God's aims in revealing his name to his people, according to Scripture, was to provide them with supernatural resources. He really wanted them to find answers to their prayers and protection in their crises by calling on their special relationship with him. "May the LORD answer you when you are in distress; may the name of the God of Jacob protect you," sings the psalmist. "Some trust in chariots and some in horses, but we trust in the name of the LORD our God" (Psalm 20:1, 7).

The name of *Jesus* is a powerful resource for Christians, too. "You may ask me for anything in my name, and I will do it," he assured his first disciples (John 14:14). And they took him at his word. Through their words and touch, God's converting, healing power revolutionized other people's lives (see Acts 4:10, 12, 16). And one day, as they forecast, every human and superhuman knee will bow in submission to the authority of Jesus' name (Philippians 2:10).

God reveals his nature as the all-loving Savior and all-powerful Lord through his name. He wants us to experience for ourselves all that his name declares him to be. So one of the most obvious ways of misusing the name of almighty God is to fail to use it as regularly and as confidently as we should.

God promises to answer powerfully when we ask humbly in his name. So why do we not pray with more trust? "Everyone who calls on the name of the Lord will be saved," declare both the Old and the New Testaments (Joel 2:32; Acts 2:21). So why do we not spread the gospel with more conviction? Timid evangelists and hesitant pray-ers are way out of line with the spirit of the third commandment.

There is, of course, a more obvious way in which the power of God's name can be misused. That is by using it selfishly. The third commandment warns us to be on our guard against that, too.

Prayer in the name of Jesus certainly releases God's power. But according to Jesus himself, the whole purpose of tapping God's resources in this way is to bring glory to him, not personal satisfaction to the person who does the praying (see John 14:13). Prayer was never intended to be used like a slot machine, with the believer putting in the right-shaped coin (the name of Jesus) in the hope of coaxing a spiritual bar of chocolate out of God as a reward. Selfish prayers that end with the formula "for Jesus' sake" are an abuse of his name.

Evangelism can involve misuse of God's name, too. The tragic cases of power-hungry, status-seeking televangelists in America show how easily it can happen. There may be nothing wrong with the gospel message that is proclaimed. Viewers may come to a genuine personal faith as a result of what they see and hear (compare Paul's experience in Philippians 1:15-18). But if the evangelist's motives are selfish—

or even mixed—the Savior's name has been seriously abused.

It is also possible to misuse God's name by claiming his approval for one's own ideas. Jeremiah knew some prophets who did exactly that by speaking their own minds and then adding, "So says God" (Jeremiah 14:15; 23:25). Two weeks ago a Christian friend for whom I have the greatest respect wrote me a note beginning, "God has told me. . . ." That is a particularly risky thing to do (and in this case it really meant, "After praying, I think the right thing to do is . . . "). In different circumstances, it might even add up to spiritual blackmail.

God wants his name to be *used*. But he will never allow it to be *owned*.

BEARING HIS REPUTATION

A couple of years ago my wife and I had a vacation in a farmhouse in Scotland. Another family (total strangers) were staying on the farm at the same time. We thought there was something a little sour and unattractive about their attitude to the farmer's wife. On the third evening, I said to my wife, "I hope they're not Christians." By the end of the week we had discovered that they were. Perhaps we were overreacting (and perhaps they had negative thoughts about us too), but in a curious way we felt God's reputation was at stake in the dynamics of that holiday.

"God's name is blasphemed . . . because of you," Paul wrote to some Jews he knew who were in the habit of breaking God's commandments (Romans 2:24). As members of God's special people, they were identified with him in others' eyes. In an illogical but understandable way, outsiders judged the validity of the Jews' God by the integrity of their behavior. If they behaved badly, it was God's reputation that suffered.

Whenever a gap develops between our beliefs and our behavior, we misuse the Lord's name when we call ourselves *Christ*ians. Paul's strong language should stop us in our tracks. People who "claim to know God, but by their actions they deny him" are, he wrote, "detestable, disobedient and unfit for doing anything good" (Titus 1:16).

That needs breaking down into practical detail. If I claim that God is in charge of everything I own, can I ask him to countersign all my checks? If I disown those "whose god is their belly," can I look the Lord in the eye when I submit last week's nondiet record to him? If I have an I Love Jesus sticker on my car, do I make other drivers curse both of us by the way I drive?

When soccer hooligans smash up a pub, the club whose colors they wear disowns them.

"We'd rather they didn't come through *our* turn-stiles," the manager says. "They're not genuine supporters at all. They simply bring disgrace on our name" (Matthew 6:9).

Jesus spoke in similar terms about men and women who misuse his name. "Not everyone who says to me, 'Lord, Lord,' will enter the kingdom of heaven," he warned them, "but only he who does the will of my Father who is in heaven." Those whose lives deny the close relationship with him that they claim will hear his chilling words, "I never knew you" (Matthew 7:21, 23). And that is an exclusion notice far, far more terrible than being shut out of a soccer stadium.

Misusing God's name is a serious health hazard in the Christian life. But there is one effective way to inoculate ourselves against that risk. "This, then, is how you should pray," taught Jesus. "Our Father in heaven, *hallowed* be your name."

Christians share Christ's intimacy with God. Like him, they can call God "Father." But the closeness they enjoy must be controlled by the distance that awe and reverence demand. If God's name is hallowed, it will not be misused.

Worship will be uninhibited, but not casual. Promises will be kept, and never evaded. His power will be used to the full, but not selfishly. And deeds will match words.

TO THINK AND TALK ABOUT

1. Why does it matter how we use God's name?

2. The author mentions the privilege of being on personal-name terms with God. How can we be intimate with him without being irreverent, and reverent without losing our intimacy? How well do you maintain the balance (a) in your own time with God, and (b) together in your church's worship?

3. What do you think is the most constructive way of relating to people who use the names of God and Jesus as swear words? Share your experiences.

4. The author believes that Christians sometimes misuse God's name in their prayers, evangelism, and understanding of God's will in particular situations. How can we avoid falling into these traps?

5. The author wrote: "Whenever a gap develops between our beliefs and our behavior, we misuse the Lord's name when we call ourselves *Christ*ians." How can we narrow the gap? Is it possible to be a consistent Christian who doesn't dishonor the Lord's name and still be a "real person" who gets things wrong and experiences negative emotions?

SIX
Balanced Living: The Fourth Commandment

Remember the Sabbath day by keeping it holy. Six days you shall labor and do all your work, but the seventh day is a Sabbath to the LORD your God. On it you shall not do any work, neither you, nor your son or daughter, nor your manservant or maidservant, nor your animals, nor the alien within your gates. For in six days the LORD made the heavens and the earth, the sea, and all that is in them, but he rested on the seventh day. Therefore the LORD blessed the Sabbath day and made it holy.
(Exodus 20:8-11)

In 1981, a film with a haunting theme tune won an Oscar. *Chariots of Fire* was all about a Chris-

tian sprinter called Eric Liddell. He was selected
to represent his country for the 1924 Olympics,
but refused to run in his main event because it
was scheduled for a Sunday. In the face of much
misunderstanding and criticism, he stuck to his
principles. And, of course, the story had a happy
ending. He won a gold medal at a different distance.

Liddell's Christian witness made him famous
overnight. But why did he refuse to run on a
Sunday? He took his stand on the fourth commandment. But did he apply it rightly?

This commandment bans *work* on the Sabbath, but unlike top athletes today, Eric never
got paid for his running. The commandment
tells us to follow God's example when he
"rested" on the seventh day, but does "resting"
rule out sprinting? And anyway, Sunday is not
the seventh day of the week. If Eric Liddell had
been a Seventh Day Adventist, he would never
have thought that competing on a Sunday was a
breach of the fourth commandment.

All Christians praise God for the fine example
of a man who had the guts to obey his conscience. But big questions still remain for the
rest of us. Is a modern Christian defying God
when he or she runs for the local team on a Sunday afternoon? And what about the minister who
goes for a jog before breakfast to get himself in

good physical condition to lead Sunday worship? Where and how do we draw the lines?

The starting point is to expand our horizons. The scope of this commandment covers much more than Sunday observance.

WORK

For one thing, it gives us a basis for arriving at a Christian approach to work.

The pattern we are to follow as we "labor and do all our work" is the one set by God the Creator himself. "The LORD made the heavens and the earth, the sea, and all that is in them." We have a God who works.

Working God. The Bible's creation teaching paints a picture of the working God in vivid human imagery.

More than once, he is described as a *manual worker.* Gazing up at the night sky, David realized that he was looking at the work of God's own hands (Psalm 8:3, 6). Isaiah had the same thought when he compared the Creator to a potter, elbow-deep in his raw material (Isaiah 45:9). Like a skilled craftsman, the Lord works with enormously delicate precision in piecing together the developing fetus, sings the psalmist. And he operates on the "macro" scale as well.

"The heavens declare the glory of God; the skies proclaim the work of his hands" (Psalm 19:1).

Sometimes, too, the Bible pictures God as an *executive worker.* The account of creation in Genesis is punctuated by the little phrase, "And God said"—followed more often than not by the terse report, "And it was so." In other words, whenever God spoke with executive authority, things happened. Once again, it is the poetic language of the Psalms that illustrates this feature of God's work most strikingly. "By the word of the LORD were the heavens made" (Psalm 33:6). "He commanded and they were created" (Psalm 148:5).

God is even represented as a worker who enjoys job satisfaction. When he surveyed various stages of his creation, he "saw that it was good." And when the work was complete, he nodded his head with divine approval: "God saw all that he had made, and it was good" (see Genesis 1:10, 12, 18, 21, 25, 31).

Even allowing for the poetic coloring, the non-Jewish world could not stomach this idea of a God who worked. Hard labor, they thought, was beneath the dignity of the Supreme Deity. He would surely not lower himself to the point where he got his hands dirty! The Greeks actually invented a "demiurge" (a semidivine clerk of works) to supervise the messy business of creation. But the Bible has no space for any demiurge. The Creator does the dirty work himself.

Working people. God made human beings in his own working image. That much is clear from the Bible's first two chapters. The very first instruction the Creator gave to man and woman invested them with breathtaking managerial responsibility. "Fill the earth and subdue it," he told them. And when they were safely installed in the Garden of Eden, the Lord instructed them "to work it and take care of it" (Genesis 2:15).

The word *work* there usually stands for physical labor, while the Hebrew expression "take care of" is more of a management term. In today's language, Adam had a dual role. He was a plantation worker and a plantation manager rolled into one.

These first human workers no doubt shared their Creator's job satisfaction. But Scripture goes into much more detail about the way they *lost* it. When they rebelled against God, we are told how sin spoiled the whole of human experience, including work.

The Bible paints yet another vivid word picture at this point of the story: "The LORD God banished him [man] from the Garden of Eden to work the ground from which he had been taken" (Genesis 3:23). In other words, the ground man and woman now worked was no longer to be in God's perfect garden. The ground on both sides of the garden fence belonged to God, of course. But the language of exclusion highlighted the gap sin had opened up between the Creator and his perfect scenario for human work on the one hand, and the spoiled environment in which man and woman actually do their work on the other.

Scripture even spells out some of the practical consequences. Although some of the language sounds quaint to us now, the underlying truths ring loud bells in our contemporary experience. In the first place, there was conflict between man and his resources: "Cursed is the ground because of you," thundered the Lord. "It will produce thorns and thistles for you" (Genesis 3:17-18). Added to that, envious conflict spoiled relationships between working people. Immediately after its account of man's rebellion against God, the Bible describes the bloody dispute between Cain and Abel, two working men fighting to the death over the products of their labor.

Above all, the arrival of sin produced conflict in man's own mind as he thought about work. What was intended to be a blessing became a pain and a nuisance. The original positive vibes were replaced by overwhelmingly negative ones. In the words of Genesis, human labor wound up as "painful toil."

Signposts. It is a big mistake, then, to limit the meaning of the fourth commandment to a list of the things God wants his people to avoid on Sundays. By taking us back to God's activity in creation, it provides us with a powerful critical analysis of modern attitudes to work.

How else can we account for the love-hate relationship to our work that many of us feel today? So long as we are doing it, we long for weekends when we can stop. (The worst thing about Sunday, as someone has wearily said, is that it is the day before Monday.) But if we lose our work through sickness or employment lay-off, we immediately scream with pain, as though an important part of us has been amputated.

The Bible's two-pronged explanation for this curious example of human doublethink has a ring of truth about it. In the first place, we need to work because we are made in the image of our working Creator. It is not just the lack of a wage that makes us ache when we are laid off from work. It is the loss of an essential part of our human makeup.

But there is a second, shadow side to our experience of work. Even when we have it, few of us find complete satisfaction in doing it. Though we might not always see the situation in these biblical terms, sin has spoiled our working environment.

So many of the jobs we do are crashing bores. We look enviously over our shoulders at those who have an easier ride (by which we often mean larger rewards for less effort). And strained relationships between management and labor (whichever side we are on) make us long for retirement, even in our thirties and forties.

The fourth commandment does at least set up some basic signposts to help us out of this maze, by pointing us to God and his instructions for man and woman.

The writing on the first signpost tells us that *work is good.* It has to be, because God does it himself. Religions that picture their supreme deity luxuriating in the work-free bliss of eternal leisure have got it all wrong. And the Creator made people to be workers, too. Human beings have been so constructed by their Maker that they cannot find personal fulfillment if they do no work.

Christians, then, begin with a positive bias toward working. A job is not just the long, dark tunnel that separates holidays. In spite of all its frustrations, work is a blessing, not a burden. A regular check from Social Security or a golden handshake from a multinational company cannot possibly compensate for the loss of it.

The second signpost points us in the direction of *job satisfaction.* God again is our model. He found total satisfaction in the work he did, and he means for us to do the same.

This provides Christians with a political platform from which to challenge modern structures that inhibit job satisfaction. We will be particularly sensitive to the symptoms of sin's poison in the industrial system, especially when we see some working people exploiting others for selfish gain.

The third signpost is even more radical. It tells us that *all work is of equal value.* In the human picture language, the Bible describes God's work as both manual labor and executive management. And in the imagery of Genesis, the first man was given work that spanned the gap between management and labor.

Here we have a direct biblical challenge to all views of work that value some occupations above others. When those with desk jobs look down their educated noses at manual workers (and those who work with their hands despise pen pushers as parasites who do not know what real work is), Christians should see bright, biblical warning lights. White collar, blue collar, or no collar—it makes no difference to God. He calls craftsmen to serve him just as much as prophets (Exodus 31:1-11).

And we must add clergy collars to the list, too. Even in the church, it is easy to slip into a pecking-order mentality when we think about work. Right at the top of the pile, we assume, are those with "vocations"—from missionaries and clergy to secretaries who work for Christian organizations. Below them come lesser mortals who have only "ordinary jobs." And down at the bottom of the list, at risk of relegation, we find people with dubious occupations like barmaids and night-club bouncers. The warning lights should be shining even more brightly when we catch ourselves making lists in our minds like that.

Our college maintenance man has a card stuck up in the window of his workshop. It reads, Carpenter from Nazareth Seeks Joiners. (Editor's note: British English enables a pun on the word *joiner,* which is another name for a furniture maker.) That is a constant reminder to me that the Son of God saw nothing inconsistent between woodwork and the work of salvation.

The fourth signpost urges us to move in the most unlikely direction of all. It encourages us to *distinguish between work and employment.*

When we think of work, we think about paid jobs. If I am not earning a wage, I am out of work—by definition.

The Bible does not see work in that narrow, myopic way at all. It certainly demands that those in wage-earning jobs should be paid justly (see Jeremiah 22:13 and James 5:4), but it never suggests that work and employment are the same thing. When God gave the first man and woman their life's work, it came with the instruction to develop and control the whole of creation, including their own fertility. He was not issuing them with unfortunately necessary passports to weekly paychecks.

If we follow this signpost boldly, we can begin to make sense of such things as unemployment, housework, and retirement. Those who earn no wages for what they do are not exempt from their Creator's mandate to manage the resources of his world. And that is what work really is.

All four of these signposts cry out for follow-up. But we are halfway through a chapter on the fourth commandment, and we have not got to Sunday yet!

REST

Although the fourth commandment has much to tell us about attitudes to work, it devotes most of its space to rest. And once again, God's own example is the focal point. The Creator "rested on the seventh day." So, says the commandment, must we.

Here we have the most daring biblical word picture of all. The idea of God working with his

hands is bold enough. But the thought of a working God who needs his rest day is almost embarrassing. As if to rub it in, a later chapter in
Exodus tells how God "abstained from work and
got his breath back" on the seventh day (Exodus
31:17). "Got his breath back" is not in any
English version I have seen, but it is exactly
what the original Hebrew expression means.
Even translators can be squeamish at times.

The whole point behind the vivid imagery, of
course, is to make sure that you and I do not
miss the vital point. God is deliberately model-
ing a human need. Whatever our work
involves—whether we love it or hate it—we
need a regular break from doing it. That is the
way we are made. As one commentator puts it,
the need for a balance in life between work and
rest is a law written into every cell of the human
body.

This is the point where we need to dig a little
more deeply into the meaning of the words at
the heart of the commandment. "Therefore the
LORD *blessed* the *Sabbath* day and made it *holy.*"

When God declares something "holy," he
takes it out of ordinary circulation. He makes it
special. It may be a holy place, reserved for worship; a holy animal, set aside for sacrifice; or a
holy day, marked out as different from the other
days of the week. So the most obvious way of

abusing a holy day is to make it ordinary, by blurring its distinctiveness.

By "blessing" the seventh day, God made his intention for its use very plain. It was to be different in a highly positive way, one of his most prized gifts to mankind. If a cloud of gloom and depression hung over the Sabbath in Bible times, something had gone badly wrong. Isaiah captures the Creator's design perfectly when he describes the Sabbath as "a delight," a day when "you will find your joy in the LORD" (Isaiah 58:13-14).

This is where the religious experts of Jesus' day went wrong. They counted up thirty-nine Hebrew letters in the original commandment, concluded that there must be thirty-nine main categories of work that were out of bounds on the Sabbath, divided each category into another thirty-nine subsections to be on the safe side, and ended up with 1,521 "Thou shalt nots." It was an ecclesiastical lawyer's dream, but everyone else's nightmare. It completely reversed the commandment's thrust. It turned a blessing into a burden. God's celebration streamers had become yards of forbidding red tape. No wonder Jesus commented, "The Sabbath was made for man, not man for the Sabbath" (Mark 2:27).

The meaning of *Sabbath* is, of course, the key. The root of the Hebrew word means "cease" or "rest." But that does not really answer the questions we want to ask. What, in practical terms, does it mean to cease or rest from our work?

The need for change. We have already seen that *work* in the Bible does not necessarily mean a paid job. It stands for whatever small (but important) share God has given us in managing the resources of his creation. Now we must turn the coin over. *Rest* cannot simply mean a break from our paid jobs. After all, some of us do not have one of those. It stands for the things God means us to do when we are not engaged in our life's main task.

In other words, in every person's life there should be a major and a minor component. And the word *every* is worth underlining. Whether I am a paid employee, a student on a grant, a housewife (or househusband) with a weekly budget to manage, an unemployed person, or someone living on a pension, it is God's will that there should be a "major" in my life. And balancing that major, there must be a "minor."

This is the Sabbath principle. It can be summed up as change. We are so made that we need variety in life. Workaholics are really little better than alcoholics. Both are abusing something that is good and God-given by overusing it. Change is part of our personal hygiene.

This is how the Old Testament treats the Sabbath law whenever it spells out its practical demands in different situations. Out in the desert, the Israelites were told to stay in their tents on the Sabbath day (Exodus 16:29). In a nomadic life-style, that was about the only change in life's routine that they could make.

In more settled times, the regulations naturally became more specific. The farmer must stop his plowing on the Sabbath, even when the weather was perfect for it (Exodus 34:21). The housewife must not cook, and the traveling salesman must put his samples down (Exodus 35:3; Jeremiah 17:27). They all needed change. Everyone needed suitable "minors" to balance the "majors," in a proportion of one to six.

The New Testament warns us not to be slavish or legalistic about keeping exactly to that 1:6 ratio. Paul writes that those who insist on observing Sabbaths, come what may, are actually taking a step backward in their spiritual lives (see Galatians 4:10 and Colossians 2:16). But the Sabbath principle remains a firm fixture for non-Christians and Christians alike. Whatever our work, we need a regular break from it. Whether or not we believe in a personal Creator, this is the way we have been made.

Some prominent Christians of the past have taken such pains to avoid laziness that they have

fallen into the trap of downgrading life's
"minors." John Wesley, for example, wrote into
the rules of a school he founded, "There will be
no games, for he that plays when a boy will play
when a man." And Charles Spurgeon was fond
of reminding his congregations how often God
appeared to men and women in Bible times
when they were working—*too* fond, perhaps,
because he conveniently forgot to mention the
numerous occasions when the Lord met people
in their sleep.

So what has all this to do with Sunday? In
some ways, not very much. The New Testament
nowhere suggests that Sunday is the Christian
Sabbath. If you are the minister of a church, Sunday cannot possibly be your Sabbath day.
Preaching and leading worship are important
parts of your "major." In order to observe the
Sabbath principle, you must take a day off during the week to pick up on your "minors."

Ministers are probably the greatest Sabbath-
breakers of all. I worked with one once. He left
his clergy collar off every Tuesday, but that
made absolutely no difference in the way he
spent his day. And I knew exactly how he felt.
My Sabbath day was Thursday at the time, and I
remember the terrible feelings of guilt I had
whenever I tried sitting in a deck chair at eleven
o'clock on a sunny Thursday morning. Out there

in the garden, I imagined the reproachful eyes of all the housewives in the surrounding flats and houses boring into my back as they muttered darkly about "one-day-a-week parsons." In reality, of course, they had far better things to do than look at me.

Even if Sunday *is* your Sabbath day, I can find no suggestion in the Bible that you need to spend it quietly. That is not what stopping work means.

God wants us to be healthy, balanced people. If our major weekday work involves a great deal of physical exertion, we will naturally need to find Sabbath occupations that ease aching muscles and stimulate the mind. But if we spend our working days sitting at a desk, then playing sport or digging in the garden may be just the right kind of Sabbath activity for us. Getting a coronary through an unbalanced life-style may well be the result of too much Sabbath breaking.

Time for worship. I realize I am being provocative. Now is the time to complete the biblical picture in a more conventional way.

The Ten Commandments appear in full not once but twice in the Old Testament. I have been using the version in Exodus. There, the rule about Sabbath keeping goes back to *creation* and to the way people have been made. The "major and minor" theme applies to everyone, not just to Christians.

The second version, in the book of Deuteronomy, phrases the fourth commandment differently. The instructions about stopping work are very similar, but the reason given for keeping the Sabbath is quite distinct. It takes us back to God's great act of *redemption* in Old Testament times: "Remember that you were slaves in Egypt and that the LORD your God brought you out of there with a mighty hand and an outstretched arm" (Deuteronomy 5:15).

As well as encouraging them to live a balanced life, in obedience to their Maker's instructions, Sabbath keeping was a constant reminder to God's people of his great love and power in liberating them from slavery. So no Sabbath was properly observed without an act of worship.

Here we have a very clear link with our observance of Sunday. Christians have a much greater act of redemption to celebrate than liberation from a political oppressor. Jesus died to free us from the grip of sin. His victory was made public on the first day of the week, when he rose from the dead. The Holy Spirit, God's guarantee of a liberated life, first filled Christian believers on the Day of Pentecost—which was also a Sunday. What could be more natural than to transfer the big day for Christian celebration, the day when Christians meet together to praise God for their redemption, from the seventh day of the week to the first?

In Old Testament times, when people worked a six-day week, the day of rest and the day of worship were one and the same. Even then, the twin purposes were kept distinct by the different versions of the Ten Commandments in Exodus and Deuteronomy. In New Testament times, as far as Christians were concerned (especially Jewish Christians), the two began to pull apart.

There are just three references in the New Testament to worship on the Lord's Day, but no hint that it was observed as a day off, like the Jewish Sabbath. The fact that one young man went to sleep in the middle of a sermon and fell out of a third-story window at midnight (Acts 20:7-12) suggests that most Sunday services took place at the end of a busy working day.

Later, Sabbath and Sunday merged, and the regulations of the fourth commandment were applied (in spite of Martin Luther's objections) to regulate Christian behavior on the first day of the week.

That, perhaps, is a pity. The virtue of keeping rest and worship separate is not only that it encourages ministers to take a day off. In times when most people work a five-day week, it also "releases" people like teachers and technicians to put their talents at the church's disposal on Sundays, without feeling that they are disobeying God's law by working on their Sabbath.

So the fourth of the Ten Commandments covers an enormous amount of ground. Highlighting God's own example, it provides guidelines for the way we define and approach our work. And it draws our attention to the need for a balanced life-style. As *human beings,* we need time and space to balance life's "majors" with appropriate "minors" by taking regular Sabbath breaks. And as *Christians,* we cannot do without the opportunities that Sunday services provide for celebrating our salvation together.

The first word of the commandment is in some ways the most important of all. We need constantly to "remember." The trees outside need no reminding about the need to take regular breaks from the business of bearing fruit. But you and I have the freedom to do nothing but work, if we want to. We need those regular Sabbath jogs to the memory.

And we know how easy it is to lose the thrill of our salvation when we drop out of regular church attendance. We need reminding about that, too. As the Puritan preacher Thomas Watson put it, Sunday worship "oils the wheels of our affections" for the God who worked so hard to save us.

TO THINK AND TALK ABOUT

1. Before we talk about Sabbath days we must talk about working days. Why do you think we *need* to work (apart from the money, or because *someone's* got to see to the kids)? What light does this commandment shed on this question? Why is it so painful to be without work?

2. Despite our need to work (for all the reasons you've just given), why do we have such an ambivalent attitude toward our work?

3. According to this commandment, why does rest matter?

4. Do you find it hard to rest? If so, why? How valid are these reasons?

5. Why does the Christian church keep Sunday as both a day of worship and a day of rest? Do you agree with the author that this, "perhaps, is a pity"? Why or why not?

6. If Sunday can't be your rest day, which day would be best for your "Sabbath"?

7. What practical steps can you take to ensure that your Sabbath is "holy" and "blessed"?

SEVEN
Bridging the Generation Gap: The Fifth Commandment

Honor your father and your mother, so that you may live long in the land the LORD your God is giving you. (Exodus 20:12)

The world is passing through troubled times. Young people of today think of nothing but themselves. They have no respect for parents or old age. They are impatient of all restraint. They talk as if they know everything, and treat our wisdom as stupidity. As for girls, they are forward, immodest, and unwomanly in speech, behavior, and dress.

Would you have trouble in dating the above outburst? It just might be a paragraph from an angry letter in yesterday's newspaper, written by a middle-aged commuter beaten by a youngster to the last seat on the bus. In actual fact, it comes from a sermon preached by a man called Peter the Hermit who lived from 1050 to 1115.

The generation gap has always been with us. Even in Jesus' day, rabbis could be heard complaining about the young people's hairstyles (too short, not too long!). And the conflict between the way young people behave and the standards their elders expect of them has continued to be a matter for keen debate ever since.

This is the problem that the fifth commandment tackles. And its message is immensely relevant, in spite of the tremendous changes that have taken place in the structures of family life since it was written.

It is worth pausing to take in the sweeping nature of those changes.

In Old Testament times, families stuck together closely. Several generations often lived under one roof. Parents were solely responsible for their children's health care and education, and there was plenty of able-bodied family support at hand to look after the sick and elderly. Divorce was known, but single-parent families were very rare. Children were considered assets, not nuisances—so the more you had of them the better. And in the home, father's rule went unchallenged.

All this seems light-years away from family life today. With clinics, day-care centers, schools, and old people's homes, life-and-death responsibilities of parents and children for one another have all but disappeared. Teenagers no longer depend on their fathers to learn the skills of a trade (in fact, father's knowledge will probably be out of date by the time they leave school). The chances are quite high that he will have walked out of the home before then anyway. And in that case, there will certainly not be any room in the two-bedroomed flat for Grandma.

When we read what the Bible has to say about family life, we have to build in these checks and balances. Nevertheless, the core issues that the fifth commandment addresses are as relevant now as they were in Old Testament society. How should young children be brought up? What are the parent's responsibilities for the child he or she has brought into the world (even if it is with the help of an anonymous sperm donor nowadays)? How should grown children treat their aging fathers and mothers? And what is the link (if any) between the health of family life and the soundness of society?

In a nutshell, how do we bridge the generation gap?

The fifth commandment has a one-word formula. *Honor,* in Hebrew, means "treat as weighty." That is not the same as "obey without question," though obedience is the most obvious way a young child will honor a parent. Nor is it identical with love. The way some parents treat their children inspires hate, not affection. The Bible is too realistic to ignore that.

Honor does not even mean "give them their due." Some elderly parents have done little or nothing to earn their adult children's gratitude.

The commandment's call for children of all ages to honor their fathers and mothers involves more than obedience, love, or gratitude. In continually shifting patterns of family relationships, it remains the one constant factor. Its demands are well worth exploring.

GROWING UP

Paul is in no doubt what honoring parents means in early childhood. As a commentary on the fifth commandment, he writes, "Children, obey your parents in the Lord, for this is right" (Ephesians 6:1; compare Colossians 3:20).

Obedience is the correct response to discipline, and being disciplined is a sign that you are really loved. That is the clear message to parents with young children in both the Old and New Testaments. The Epistle to the Hebrews even uses discipline in the home to illustrate God's love for his people. "We have all had human

fathers who disciplined us and we respected
them for it. How much more should we submit
to the Father of our spirits and live!" (Hebrews
12:9).

If the author of this New Testament letter had
been writing today, he might not have been quite
so optimistic about discipline in the average
home. Many modern parents, aided and abetted
by theories that children are happiest when they
are allowed to express themselves most freely,
keep discipline to a minimum.

I think of a girl I once knew called Shona. She
very nearly joined our church's young people's
group. But she never quite made it. She drifted
into a different crowd instead and got heavily
involved in the local drug scene. One morning
her body was found dumped in a park about a
mile from her home. She had been strangled by
a young man, after she had taunted him for fail-
ing to have intercourse with her successfully.

My heart went out to her. What had gone
wrong? It could have happened to anyone, but
when I visited her parents I think I found out
why Shona had been particularly at risk. For
years she had enjoyed a degree of freedom that
her friends must have envied. There was absolutely no discipline in her home. She had no reason to become a rebel because there was nothing
to rebel against. No questions were asked about

the time she came in at night, or about the nights when she never came in at all. And she had no difficulty in covering up her drug taking.

The moment that really broke her mother's heart was when a half-written note was found in her bedroom, asking for an appointment to talk things over. It came too late. She had already found the "freedom" to die in the long grass a few days after her sixteenth birthday.

Shona's case notes make a sad commentary on the home truth set out so tersely in the Old Testament's book of Proverbs (with the gender adjusted): "Discipline your [daughter], for in that there is hope; do not be a willing party to [her] death" (Proverbs 19:18). Parents who pamper their children are leading them along a deadly path. The right pattern, according to Scripture, is for firm family rules that call for clear-cut obedience.

The book of Proverbs is also outspoken in advocating corporal punishment when those rules are broken. "Children just naturally do silly, careless things, but a good spanking will teach them how to behave" (Proverbs 22:15, TEV). "Don't hesitate to discipline a child. A good spanking won't kill him" (Proverbs 23:13, TEV).

This, of course, is highly controversial. It is the point where many modern parents want to draw back from the Bible in alarm. Enforced obedience may well be in a child's best interests. But is it right to hit them?

Bruised young faces staring out at us blankly from the pages of our newspapers warn us how easily such discipline can sink into bad-tempered violence. I have such a press photograph in front of me now. Little Doreen Mason was brutally treated by her father and mother. Her left leg was broken in five places by repeated blows. Witnesses reported that tears welled up in the toddler's eyes when her mother hit her, but she never cried out aloud because she was afraid. She died as the result of a fractured skull, a tragic testimony to the fact that a good whipping *can* sometimes kill. And in the London borough where she lived, eighteen out of every thousand children are known to be physically abused by their parents.

That, of course, is brutal bullying, not the loving discipline the Old Testament advocates. In his letter to Christians at Colosse, Paul is careful to balance his call for children to obey with a warning to parents not to abuse their power. "Fathers, do not embitter your children, or they will become discouraged" (Colossians 3:21).

The word Paul chooses there for "embitter" was also used for challenging an opponent to a boxing match. That is why bullying is quite different from firm discipline. The home is not a boxing ring. These "opponents" are not even fairly matched. The father who picks quarrels with his children, demanding their obedience "or else," is a cruel sadist. Martin Luther had a father just like that. It meant that for many years he could not pray to God as Father. "Spare the rod and spoil the child, it is true," he wrote later on; "but beside the rod keep an apple to give him when he does well."

Parents who pamper their children by withholding discipline are doing them no good at all. And those who tyrannize their families are worse. Good parents are those who tread the tightrope between these two extremes by insisting, in love, that basic rules are kept.

BECOMING INDEPENDENT

So when you are young, *honor* means "obey." But what happens as you get older—when the time comes to think about leaving home? Does God continue to demand unquestioning obedience then?

The Bible's answer to that is a clear no. Jesus' own example is important here. As a boy, he obeyed Joseph and Mary (though there was a misunderstanding about his "father" when he got lost at the age of twelve—see Luke 2:41-52). But once he embarked on his ministry as a mature adult, there were certainly times when he firmly refused to go along with his mother's wishes (see, for example, Matthew 12:46-50).

According to the Bible, there are two special turning points in life when your parents' desires for you must take second place. The first comes when you discover what God wants you to do with your future. Jesus made that unmistakably clear himself. If God's will and your parents' wishes pull you in opposite directions, there can be no argument who should win. "I have come to turn 'a man against his father, a daughter against her mother,'" warned Jesus. "Anyone who loves his father or mother more than me is not worthy of me" (Matthew 10:35, 37).

The second milestone comes when (and if) you decide to marry. Getting married means that you break the old-style bond with your parents in order to forge a new one with your husband or wife. Again, the Bible leaves us in no doubt whose wishes should prevail if your partner and your parents disagree about a big decision that has to be made in married life (see Genesis 2:24).

This is possibly what Paul meant when he instructed children to obey their parents "in the Lord" (Ephesians 6:1). A young adult's right to make decisions must be respected. If God pulls you firmly one way, "We know best" is an inadequate counterargument from parents who want to push you in the opposite direction. William Barclay explains it very well. "The great and difficult task of parenthood," he wrote, "is to exercise control in such a way that in the end the child will not need it any more."

Some parents, with the best motives in the world, are too possessive for too long. I know. My own father and mother had a career in the Foreign Office mapped out for me. They steered me through school to the university, and I am glad they forced me to do my homework when I wanted to do other things. But eventually I got serious about a girl they considered "unsuitable," and then God called me to get ordained. My father did everything he could to stop me from getting engaged, and my mother refused to go out of the house for some time in case a neighbor happened to ask her what I was planning to do when I left the university.

It was a blatant but very understandable form of blackmail. I am enormously glad that I stood out against my parents on both counts. But I am ashamed, when I look back, by the conceited and uncaring way in which I did it.

The passing of the years marks the end of obedience. But it does not make the command to "honor" parents obsolete. *Honor,* remember, means "treat as weighty." I could at least have

listened with respect to my parents' arguments—
and tried to understand them—instead of preaching to them proudly in their own kitchen.

CARE OF THE ELDERLY

Abuse of family power takes on a completely fresh complexion when parents get old. Their children are now the strong ones. The dependency roles are reversed. And the generation gap takes on a new and even more sinister shape.

The Bible warns adult children not to treat their frail parents with contempt. The elderly must not be discarded as a nuisance. The fifth commandment still applies. "Cursed is the man who *dis*honors his father or his mother," cautions the Old Testament law (Deuteronomy 27:16, emphasis mine). Whether the blows are physical or verbal, no adult child may ever use his or her superior strength to strike out against a parent (see Exodus 21:15, 17).

By Jesus' day, abuse had taken on a more sophisticated form. There was a legal fiction that allowed grown-up children to opt out of their financial responsibilities for aging mothers and fathers. By declaring their assets *Corban* (which meant "belonging to God"), they could effectively deprive their parent of the material support they needed. Jesus quoted the fifth commandment to expose such hypocrisy. What an outrageous way to evade your duty to "honor" those who brought you into the world, by building a bypass around God's command in God's own name (Mark 7:9-13)!

As always, Jesus matched his teaching with action. When he hung from the cross on Good Friday, he saw his grief-stricken mother watching him die. With the sin of the world on his shoulders, he summoned up the strength to make sure that she would have a roof over her head when he was gone (John 19:25-27).

Honoring an elderly parent is as practical as that. It often involves a great deal of sacrifice. Banishing a frail mother to an old people's home, where she will be fed, kept warm, and left to vegetate in a lonely armchair, may be the exact reverse of honoring her.

Here, however, we must remember the difference between Bible times and our own, and exercise a little caution. Few of us have the resources of an extended family (or the space) to spread the burden of care. Having an elderly relative live with you in a small flat can break your marriage and wreck the fragile relationships of a nuclear family. It may make him or her feel very unhappy, too. In some cases, there may be better options. The really important thing is the honoring, not the geography. Whether parents wind up in granny flats or in geriatric units, there are always ways and means of making them know they are loved and respected.

That is the bottom line. No Christian can evade it with a clear conscience. As the New Testament says, "If anyone does not provide for his relatives, and especially for his immediate family, he has denied the faith and is worse than an unbeliever" (1 Timothy 5:8).

The traffic is by no means all one-way, however. The older still have much to contribute to the younger.

From the economic point of view, it is true that the elderly may be a drag. The Bible is very frank about that. In monetary terms, the Old Testament law calculates that the over-sixties have lost two-thirds of their value (see Leviticus 27:1-7). But productivity is not everything. Looking after elderly people may interfere with the business of making money, but their contribution to the community in other ways is extremely valuable. In Bible times, their advice was sought and respected, on the assumption that it was likely to be better informed and more balanced than that of the younger generation. And the role of grandparents in the bringing up of children was greatly prized.

Grandparents today may live hundreds of miles away from their children's children. In our modern, highly mobile Western society, we have almost lost the sense of extended family altogether. This is perhaps a more damaging social change than we have yet acknowledged.

In a House of Lords debate on the family, a former archbishop of Canterbury quoted from an essay written by an eight-year-old boy on "What a Grandmother Is." This young fellow obviously knew.

> A grandmother is a lady who has no children of her own, so she likes other people's little girls and boys. A grandfather is a man grandmother. He goes for walks with the boys and they talk about fishing and tractors. Grandmothers don't have to do anything but be there. They are old, so they shouldn't play hard or run. They should never say, "Hurry up." Usually they are fat, but not too fat to tie children's shoes. They wear glasses and funny underwear, and they can take their teeth and gums off. They don't have to be smart, only answer questions like why dogs hate cats and why God isn't married. They don't talk baby talk like visitors. When they read to us, they don't skip bits, or mind if it is the same story over again. Everybody should have one, especially if you don't have tele-

vision, because grandmothers are the only
grown-ups who have time.

THE SOCIAL DIMENSION

The fifth commandment ends with a promise.
Those who honor father and mother will "live
long in the land."

Scholars debate whether those words were
directed at individual sons and daughters, promising them a ripe old age, or at society as a
whole, guaranteeing long life to the community
that respects the values of family life.

The answer is probably both. In days when
there were no public welfare services to plug the
gaps left by parents or children who could not
(or would not) meet their family responsibilities,
it was highly likely that people who were best
"honored" would live longest. But at the same
time, the social consequences of obeying this
and the Lord's other commandments are set out
very clearly in the Old Testament. "Keep his
decrees and commands, which I am giving you
today," Moses told the whole nation, "so that it
may go well with you and your children after
you and that you may live long in the land the
LORD your God gives you for all time" (Deuteronomy 4:40).

The truth is that the Bible sees a much closer

link between the health of family life and the well-being of society than we do.

Only very recently has British law conceded that rape can occur within marriage. And even as I write this, there is a major news item on the radio reporting that British police officers are being encouraged for the first time to arrest husbands who are caught physically abusing their wives. Traditionally, these things have been viewed as "domestic disputes," private affairs in which the law of the land should not intervene.

It would have seemed very odd in Old Testament times to divide so sharply between the "private" interests of the family and the "public" concerns of the wider community. One little phrase, which choruses its way through much of the Bible, expresses the identity of the two very vividly.

In the Creation story, when the Lord made woman, man exclaimed, "This is now bone of my bones and flesh of my flesh" (Genesis 2:23). That is a lovely description of the intimacy a married couple enjoys. But the same phrase—"bone of bones and flesh of flesh"—reappears farther on in the Bible to describe relationships that seem very different to us. We find a man called Abimelech, for example, describing his extended family in bone-and-flesh language (see Judges 9:1-2). And all the tribes of Israel identified in the same close way with their king. "We are your own flesh and blood," they assured David (2 Samuel 5:1).

That is not just an interesting sociological point of difference between two kinds of community. It implies sharp criticism of societies like our own, where individualism has taken such a hold that it sounds odd to express warm closeness to your aunts and uncles (let alone your in-laws), and very odd indeed to feel a bond of intimacy between yourself and your political leaders. Could we call our prime minister or our president "bone of our bones and flesh of our flesh" and still keep a straight face?

According to the Bible, there are two special ways in which obedience to the fifth commandment makes an impact on society. It leads to a healthy respect for authority. And it also helps to reinforce important social values.

Crime and the home. The most recent set of British crime statistics backs up the first of those two points. Crime is on the increase among young teenagers on the British mainland, and it is rising most sharply in areas where family breakdowns are most common. In Northern Ireland, where family life is at its most secure, there are far fewer offenses—in spite of all the sectarian violence. And in Jewish communities, the crime rate is lowest of all. Stuart Blanch, a former bishop of Liverpool and the author of a splendid book on the Ten Commandments, tells how the governor of the Liverpool city jail used to comment with surprise whenever he received a young Jewish inmate.

That comparison would not have surprised an Old Testament criminologist. The very worst social menaces were the youngsters who rebelled against parental control (see Deuteronomy 21:18-21). Then, as now, unruly children became unruly citizens. And the reverse was true as well. Children who learned the value of order in their homes found fewest problems in respecting the authorities of their community when they grew up.

William Barclay preserves a fascinating circular once issued by the police department in Houston, Texas, making the same point. Headed, "How to Make a Child into a Delinquent," it sets out twelve easy rules.

1. Begin at infancy to give the child everything he wants. In this way, he will grow up to believe the world owes him a living.

2. When he picks up bad language, laugh at him. This will make him think he's cute.

3. Never give him any spiritual training. Wait

until he is twenty-one, and then let him decide for himself.

4. Avoid the use of the word *wrong*. It may develop a guilt complex in him. This will condition him to believe later, when he is arrested for stealing a car, that society is against him and he is being persecuted.

5. Pick up everything he leaves lying around— books, shoes, clothes. Do everything for him so that he will be experienced in throwing all responsibility on others.

6. Let him read any printed matter he can get his hands on. Be careful that the drinking glasses are sterilized, but let his mind feast on garbage.

7. Quarrel frequently in the presence of your children. In this way they will not be too shocked when the home is broken up later.

8. Give a child all the spending money he wants. Never let him earn his own. Why should he have things as tough as you had them?

9. Satisfy his every craving for food, drink, and comfort. See that every sensual desire is gratified. Denial may lead to harmful frustration.

10. Take his part against neighbors, teachers,

and policemen. They are prejudiced against your child.

11. When he gets into real trouble, apologize for yourself by saying, "I could never do anything with him."

12. Prepare for a life of grief. You will be likely to have it.

Values and the home. Hidden only just beneath the surface of this recipe for delinquency is a set of positive social values that life in the home can solidly reinforce. And that, too, is a note the Bible strikes loudly and often.

Christian fathers, writes Paul, have more to do than make sure their children grow up strong, healthy, and well qualified. They must "bring them up in the training and instruction of the Lord" (Ephesians 6:4). As well as feeding the bodies and nourishing the minds, parents are responsible for training the characters of their youngsters.

The Old Testament went even further. It encouraged graffiti. God's commandments were to be written upon the doorposts of the home, so no youngster could grow up without knowing the difference between right and wrong (see Deuteronomy 6:4-9).

This biblical approach is miles away from the

modern liberal view that parents should wrap their kids in protective cotton wool until they get mature enough to make their own minds up about life's values. Children in Bible times honored their parents by accepting their standards.

They were, of course, free to reject those standards and values later. But the chances were that as they got older they would see more and more clearly what good sense their parents' principles made. As the book of Proverbs confidently puts it, "Train a child in the way he should go, and when he is old he will not turn from it" (Proverbs 22:6).

It is the Bible's strong conviction that sound values learned in the environment of the home will make for social stability. The stronger's sense of obligation toward the weaker will inevitably show through in the shaping of political policies. Qualities like mercy and forgiveness will inform debates on penology. Self-sacrificial care of Grandma will encourage respect for all elderly people.

The opposite applies too, of course. A home life that expresses a constant struggle for power will produce selfish, power-hungry members of the community. As Stuart Blanch crisply puts it, "What happens behind our smart front door does not just dispose us as a family to happiness or misery. It is either renewing or destroying the whole community to which we belong."

The biblical idea of honor, then, straddles the generation gap. It is a prescription for resolving the tensions between young and old, not a magic formula to make them disappear. And, like a pebble dropped into a pond, its ripples spread beyond the family into society as a whole.

TO THINK AND TALK ABOUT

1. "When you are young," writes the author, "*honor* means 'obey.'" Do you agree? What responsibility does this place on parents?

2. How can parents tread the tightrope between pampering their children and tyrannizing them?

3. Young adults are no longer required to *obey* their parents, but must still *honor* them. How can they show this honor, even when they disagree on important matters such as the choice of a career or husband/wife?

4. Perhaps your parents are elderly and physically or mentally infirm. What forms can your "honoring" take in these circumstances?

5. The author believes that obedience to this commandment is good for society. Some

might see it as putting a damper on the youth-
ful questioning and self-expression that contribute to society's progress. What is your
view? (You could tackle this as a role-play
with people arguing the case for each side.)

6. Does this commandment still apply when (for
instance) your mother neglected you or your
father abused you? How can one honor such
parents?

EIGHT
Kinds of Killing: The Sixth Commandment

You shall not murder. (Exodus 20:13)

Some medical students were attending a seminar on abortion. The lecturer presented them with a case study.

"The father of the family has syphilis," she began, "and the mother TB. They have four children already. The first is blind, the second died, the third is deaf and dumb, and the fourth has TB. The mother is now pregnant with her fifth child and is willing to have an abortion if that is what you suggest. What would your advice be?"

The students voted by a large majority that the pregnancy should be terminated. "Congratulations," commented the lecturer. "You have just murdered Beethoven."

That incident sets the sixth commandment in

its modern context very starkly. Does the gynecologist commit homicide when he aborts a fetus? And does his colleague in the geriatric unit become a murderer whenever she diagnoses brain death and switches off the ventilator that is keeping a patient's heart beating?

Advances in technology have blurred the edges of our moral judgments when it comes to taking or preserving life. The experts even disagree among themselves about the exact point where life begins and death starts. The sixth commandment sounds so simple and straightforward. But applying it to the life-and-death decisions made every day in our twentieth-century hospitals is far from easy.

In actual fact, this commandment has always posed problems. Scholars have puzzled for years over the connection between its veto on killing and the Old Testament's acceptance of capital punishment and war. Does the Bible encourage us to agree to some kinds of killing, while banning others?

Most would say yes to that. The distinction is reflected in the way the commandment itself is usually translated. If you have an old Bible, it probably says, "Thou shalt not kill." But nearly all modern versions read, "You shall not murder." The assumption is that not all killing is bad, because not all killing is murder.

This is helpful. If murder means the unlawful, malicious killing of another person, it is hard to brand a gynecologist as a murderer when she terminates pregnancies lawfully and operates out of genuine concern for the well-being of her adult patient.

Unfortunately, even this useful distinction begins to crack when you apply a little more pressure. Bible words are important, and it is true that the word for "kill" in the sixth commandment (*rasah* in Hebrew) usually means the violent murder of a personal enemy. But not always. It can also be used of a lawful execution (as in Numbers 35:30). And it sometimes covers the kind of unintentional killing that the Old Testament recognizes as a noncapital offense (see Deuteronomy 4:41-42, for example).

If we really want to understand the full force of this commandment, we must dig a little deeper.

THE VALUE OF LIFE

Let's put killing to one side for the moment and focus on living.

The value the Bible sets on all human life is awesomely impressive. It rests on two fundamental facts.

The first is that *all life is God's gift*. To the modern playwright's question, "Whose life is it anyway?" the Bible's blunt answer is, "Not yours!" "Man's days are determined," observed Job in the middle of all his suffering. "You have decreed the number of his months and have set limits he cannot exceed" (Job 14:5). "When you take away their breath, [people] die and return to the dust," echoes the psalmist. "When you send your Spirit, they are created, and you renew the face of the earth" (Psalm 104:29-30).

God's gift does not come without strings. He makes us trustees, not owners, of life. So when Abel was murdered, his blood cried out to his Creator from the ground (Genesis 4:10). Cain had robbed his brother of God's property.

The second great biblical fact on which the value of human life depends is that *God made man and woman in his own image* (Genesis 1:26-27). Here is the distinguishing mark of all that it means to be human. Far above our capacity to reason, or any other feature that distinguishes people from animals, is the Bible's bewildering statement that the Creator has stamped all human beings uniquely with his own likeness.

In the euthanasia debate, well-meaning people sometimes ask why we should not act as mercifully toward human beings as we do toward animals. If it is right to put kitty out of her misery with a compassionate injection, why not Grandma? The answer is simply that kitty does not bear God's image. Human life and animal life just cannot be put on the same level. In the striking words of Thomas Watson, the Puritan preacher, taking Grandma's life would be like "tearing God's picture."

All life is God's gift, bestowed in trust. And human life is distinct, made in his image. Put those two biblical statements together and we have the fundamental reason why the life of every human being should be protected. The enemy soldier's life is worth as much as yours, even if you are fighting against him on the right side in a just war. And the life of the geriatric patient with Alzheimer's disease is as precious as the most brilliant young brain surgeon's.

All killing is bad. That is what the sixth commandment is telling us loudly and clearly. The commandment itself is God's guardrail, set up to protect his most precious gift—the gift of life.

LESSER-EVIL CHOICES

What, then, are we to make of the Bible's own insistence that life can be taken in punishment and war?

The answer lies in another vital biblical principle. In this sin-soaked world, situations can arise when the only choice we have is between doing something bad and doing something worse. Sometimes we have to choose between staying in the frying pan or jumping into the fire. There is simply nowhere else to go.

This is known as the "lesser-evil" principle. The Bible is full of it. Abraham, for example, was faced with two agonizing alternatives when God told him to sacrifice Isaac. He could either kill his son or disobey his Lord. In the end he was let off that particular hook, but only after he had made his heartbreaking decision.

Rahab was not quite so fortunate. When the Jericho police knocked on her door and asked whether she knew the whereabouts of two Israelite spies, she was faced (like Corrie ten Boom sheltering Jews in the Second World War) with the choice between telling a lie or sacrificing lives. This time there was no God-provided escape route, so she made her lesser-evil decision. "They went that way," she said, pointing to the hills—though she knew full well that the men were hiding on her roof.

Modern life, too, bristles with the need to make lesser-evil choices. In 1938, a fourteen-year-old girl was walking past a guards' barracks in London when a soldier asked whether she would like to see a horse with a green tail. "Yes, please," she said. But once inside she was viciously raped by a group of soldiers. Some time later she was admitted to the hospital in deep distress, and found to be pregnant.

Put yourself in the place of the doctor in charge of her case. What should he do?

He felt he only had three options. The first was to terminate the girl's pregnancy (which was then illegal). The second was to insist, at grave risk to her mental health, that she should go to full term for her unborn child's sake. And the third was to ask another doctor to take over.

He rejected that last "solution" as escapism. And after weighing the other two options, he chose the first. He aborted the fetus, and then reported himself to the police. He knew he had done something bad, but he believed the alternatives were worse. Some would criticize him for making the wrong choice, but few would deny that he had the responsibility to choose. In other words (and it does sound very odd), you can do something *bad*—and be *right* as you do it. That is not playing silly games with words. It is the only biblical way out of many a moral dilemma.

It is also the way to understand and apply the sixth commandment. Killing people is always bad. But in a very few extreme situations it may be the right thing to do. The Bible mentions two such sets of circumstances. If a capital crime has been committed, or if war has been declared, it may be right to kill. With our eyes on some modern dilemmas, we may want to add to that short list. But we will do so with immense caution. It is always right to choose the lesser evil, but only when we are quite sure that all the alternatives are worse.

Now, notice what this important principle is *not* saying. It does not pretend that things like killing and lying are morally neutral, bad in some situations and good in others. Rahab's lie remained bad, even though she was right to tell it. All lies are always bad. She had no need to repent afterwards (because you only need to repent when you have done the *wrong* thing), but she had every reason to regret having to be deceitful. Being forced into a lesser-evil choice is never a matter for rejoicing.

In the same kind of way, all killing is always bad. This is what the sixth commandment is telling us. It is not suggesting that we should draw up two lists, one of bad killing (like murder) and one of good (like capital punishment). The jolly executioner and the soldier who rejoices when he watches the enemy fall have both misunderstood the nature of their jobs. What they have to do may occasionally be right, but taking another person's life can never be good. The day they begin enjoying their work should be the day they stop doing it.

This, I believe, is the most helpful way Christians can tackle the life-and-death issues that hit the headlines today. We shall not always agree with one another when we debate things like capital punishment, nuclear war, and abortion. But we can at least begin from the same bottom line. Taking human life is always bad. Yet in some circumstances—all of them very regrettable—it may still be right.

Capital punishment. The Bible repeatedly echoes the sixth commandment's ban on murder. Giving life is something God loves to do. Snatching it away is playing the devil. "He was a murderer from the beginning," observed Jesus, referring to Satan (John 8:44).

There are more ways of murdering a person in real life than all the crafty devices we read about in Agatha Christie novels. The Bible recognizes that. David did away with Uriah by writing a letter; Jezebel used the processes of law to kill Naboth by remote control; and ruthless businessmen deprived debtors of their livelihood by seizing the tools of their trade (2 Samuel 11:14-15; 1 Kings 21:8-13; Deuteronomy 24:6). It would not be hard to find modern parallels to all those biblical stratagems. And we might want to add drug dealing and drunken driving to the list.

Jesus, of course, was still more radical. He traced murder back to its roots in the mind and heart. Smoldering rage and insulting words, he pointed out, are only a step away from lethal blows (Matthew 5:21-22; 15:19; see also 1 John 3:15).

The law of the land can only deal with actions and words. It cannot cope with feelings and attitudes. That is why Jesus' warning about anger and hatred cannot be reflected in the statute book. But the act of murder itself is top of most states' list of crimes. And the Bible has no doubt about the appropriate penalty. "Whoever sheds the blood of man, by man shall his blood be shed; for in the image of God has God made man" (Genesis 9:6). Those who take other people's lives have forfeited their own right to live.

In deciding how offenders should be punished, three factors must be kept in mind at the same time. First, the punishment must fit the *crime.* Secondly, it should help toward reforming the *criminal.* And thirdly, the penalty should protect the *community* by deterring the guilty person (and others) from committing similar offenses in the future.

Capital punishment for murder clearly meets the first need. If I take someone else's life, the most obvious just penalty is to lose mine in return.

That does, of course, assume that the person

charged has been justly convicted. The jury's mistake cannot be rectified afterward!

Some time ago, four Irishmen were found guilty of planting a bomb in a public house in the small town of Guildford. Several people died in the blast. All four were jailed for life. Years later, an inquiry raised grave doubts about the way the evidence against those men was collected and used. Following their release from prison, a retired judge suggested that all the fuss could have been avoided if they had been hanged after conviction. That is a chilling suggestion. Instead of supporting the case for capital punishment (as the judge intended), it surely raises serious doubts about sentencing any convicted murderer to death.

Arguments still rage about the deterrent effect of the death penalty (the third factor in punishment). Generally speaking, those most at risk—policemen and prison officers—believe that the prospect of the noose or the electric chair does deter potential killers. Others (including some psychiatrists who have spent time talking to murderers) are convinced that it does not.

There can be little argument, however, that the case for capital punishment is at its weakest when we consider the second factor—the reform of the criminal. True, living in the death-row cell can "concentrate the mind wonderfully." Some marvelous stories of pre-execution conversions are told (none better than that in Luke 23:40-43). But it does seem senseless to suggest that a murderer can best be rehabilitated by being executed.

So where does all this leave us? Looking at the crime of murder through those trifocals, it is hard to come to a firm conclusion about capital punishment. Focusing on the crime (and possibly on the community), we are pulled in one direction. With our eyes on the criminal's needs, we are pulled in the other.

It is here that the lesser-evil principle helps, by forcing us to ask other questions. If we start from the bottom line (that taking any human life is always *bad*), what kind of circumstances can make capital punishment *right?* Two obvious answers are: when no other available punishment satisfies the demands of justice, and when the life of the community is gravely at risk.

This seems to have been the principle that operated in Old Testament times. God deliberately reprieved the first murderer, and the punishment he substituted for the death penalty was clearly very appropriate (see Genesis 4:10-16). But in the state of Israel (at a time when prisons were virtually unknown) there was no alternative penalty that would fit the crime of murder. And the community would have been seriously at risk if capital punishment had been abolished.

This also helps to explain why the Old Testament lays down the death penalty for crimes other than murder. If rebellious young people threatened the community's existence—and there was no other way to counter the threat—they must die (Deuteronomy 21:18-21). And, because Israel was God's unique vehicle for revealing religious truth (in a way no state is today), blatant idolatry and blasphemy were punishable by death as well. It was less evil for the idolater to perish (evil though that was) than for God's chosen people to be fatally contaminated.

The lesser-evil principle does not provide us with a set of fail-safe answers for every different situation. But it does make us ask the right questions.

Making war. The Bible sanctions killing in war, but we need to tread extra cautiously before using biblical proof texts to justify war today. For one thing, most of Israel's fighting in Old Testament times came under the heading of *holy* war, directly ordered by God. Islamic states still fight religious wars, but Christians do not. Jesus banned his followers from taking up arms either to defend him or to spread his gospel (see Matthew 26:51-54; John 18:36). The Christian way to deal with "infidels" is to love them, not kill them. The medieval Crusades were therefore a colossal theological and historical mistake.

Equally important, modern wars are fought with very different means. Nuclear and chemical weapons have changed the whole nature of warfare. The difference, many would say, is one of kind, not just of degree.

Nevertheless, Christians from Augustine's time to our own have stoutly defended the concept of *just* war. Providing the cause is a just one, the argument goes, and the means used are not out of all proportion to the goal in view, war is best understood as an extension of policing. Just as policemen can legitimately use force to restrain muggers, so soldiers are justified in fighting international bullies.

Justice is certainly a major biblical principle. The picture of God as a righteous judge is one that the Bible draws over and over again. The Old Testament describes in the most explicit language how the Lord uses war to put injustice to rights. And in the New Testament Paul pictures the civil authorities of the state as "God's servant" who "does not bear the sword for nothing . . . to bring punishment on the wrongdoer" (Romans 13:1-4).

Even Jesus, the Prince of Peace, did not hesitate to use force when justice demanded it. To stop tradesmen from exploiting visitors to the temple, he lashed out with a whip (Mark 11:15-17)—though not, admittedly, with a machine gun or an Exocet missile.

Pacifists read the Bible very differently. They focus on the love of God and conclude that loving enemies must rule out killing them. The Old Testament forecast that the coming Messiah would be totally against war. "He . . . will settle disputes for strong nations far and wide," prophesied Micah. "Nation will not take up sword against nation, nor will they train for war anymore" (Micah 4:3). And when Jesus finally came, he fitted that description of God's Messiah perfectly in his attitude to war and violence.

Although at least one member of his inner circle of twelve was a terrorist freedom-fighter, Jesus deliberately rejected the role of political revolutionary (John 6:15). When Peter tried to defend him with a sword in the Garden of Gethsemane, he would not allow it (John 18:10-11). And he asked God's pardon for his executioners while they were still hammering the nails into his hands (Luke 23:34).

Are pacifists, then, people who put love before justice? And are those who reject pacifism people who place the demands of justice above love? The distinction is a little too sharp and simple, but it does serve to highlight the two main biblical principles at stake. God's love and justice met on Good Friday when Jesus died on the cross. And modern Christians must try to satisfy the demands of both justice and love when they discuss the merits and demerits of going to war.

Again, it is the lesser-evil principle that helps us to resolve the dilemma. The sixth commandment marks out the starting point for everybody. *All killing is bad.* Taking an enemy's life, therefore, can only be justified as an exception to that rule. Those of us who cannot accept the pacifist's position in every international dispute have to argue, "Although it is always a *bad* thing to kill, going to war in this particular situation is the *right* thing to do because all the alternatives are worse."

Applying the lesser-evil principle will not do away with disagreements among Christians at a stroke. But it will help us to understand those who differ from us in the conclusions they draw. Above all, it will ensure that we all strive for peace, whether we approve of war or not, and never exult in the death of our fellow men and women.

In 1945, a nuclear bomb was dropped on Hiroshima, and 71,139 people lost their lives. When the successful air crew returned, someone threw a celebration party for them in Washington. The centerpiece at the party was a huge iced cake, shaped like a nuclear explosion.

The captain of the crew was invited to cut the cake. He did so, but with obvious reluctance. And he was right to feel acutely embarrassed. As Joy Davidman points out in *Smoke on the Mountain,* that cake was an obscenity. It may have been right, on lesser-evil grounds, to drop the bomb (though many would dispute that). But even if it was right, it was bad. And all evil— even lesser evil—is to be regretted, not celebrated.

Abortion. Can the lesser-evil principle help us to resolve the abortion issue, too? It can, but with one important proviso.

If the fetus is treated as an unborn child with full human rights (that is the proviso), it is hard to see how abortion can ever be justified. If you doubt that, try finishing the sentence, "Although it is always a *bad* thing to kill a child, it becomes the *right* thing to do when . . . "

Most arguments for terminating a pregnancy fall to pieces when this "lesser-evil" test is applied. If you put a person's life in the scales, then health and convenience (whether of mother, family, or baby) cannot possibly tip the balance in favor of killing. We have reached the bottom line, spelled out so simply in the sixth command-

ment. That is not to play down the degree of suffering involved in having a baby in difficult circumstances, or the amount of care that ought to
be generously provided during pregnancy and
after birth. It is simply to underline the supreme
value of human life.

The only situation in which a decision to
abort may be right, on these lesser-evil grounds,
is when the presence of the fetus threatens its
mother's life (if cervical cancer has been diag-
nosed, for example). In those very rare "life ver-
sus life" situations, the woman's existing
responsibilities to her husband and family may
justify a termination—but only with her consent.

The British Parliament has recently passed a
bill that allows experiments to be performed on
human embryos less than fourteen days old. One
of the most persuasive arguments advanced by
the bill's supporters was that such experiments
would aid research into infertility and genetic
disease.

I listened to the discussion on my car radio,
and I heard one member of parliament shout
above the din of debate, "If we will the end, we
must will the means." My blood ran cold. That
was the argument the Nazis used in the Second
World War to justify their experiments on Jews
in the concentration camps. Taking some
people's lives in order to benefit other people

(however great that benefit may be) is an appalling breach of the sixth commandment.

The main reason why the bill was passed was that most members of parliament were convinced that a thirteen-day-old embryo is not a person. And the chief ground for allowing abortion is the belief that a fetus is not a baby. If the fetus that a woman carries in her womb is no more a person than her appendix, she clearly has every right to decide whether it should be removed or not.

This is the crucial point in the abortion debate. Some have tried to identify a particular moment when the embryo or fetus becomes a person. The fourteenth day (by which time the so-called "primitive streak" has appeared), the experience of quickening (when the woman is first aware of movement in her womb), and the point of viability (when the fetus is first able to survive outside its mother's womb) are the prime candidates.

Others, not convinced that these events mark anything more than milestones along the road of the unborn child's growth, prefer to speak in terms of "developing value." The earlier the stage of fetal development, the less of a person there is to be considered if an abortion is planned.

Christians cry out for biblical guidance.

Unfortunately, though not surprisingly, there is no knock-down text that provides a fail-safe answer. What the Bible does do is assume that human personhood is a continuous affair, on either side of birth. The psalmist sings (in poetic language) about God's active relationship with him in the womb (Psalm 139). Ecclesiastes advises reverent agnosticism: "As you do not know the path of the wind, or how the body is formed in a mother's womb, so you cannot understand the work of God, the Maker of all things" (Ecclesiastes 11:5). And Luke (who was, of course, a medical man) happily uses exactly the same Greek word (*brephos*) to describe both the unborn John in Elizabeth's womb and the newborn Jesus in the manger at Bethlehem (Luke 1:41, 44; 2:12, 16).

This biblical language gives no support to either of the views spelled out above. To link the arrival of personhood with some critical point in fetal development seems very arbitrary; and the "developing value" theory provides us with no basis at all for concluding with any certainty that early abortions do not kill people.

It is far better to describe the earliest embryo as a person with potential than as a potential person. And if that is true, the lesser-evil principle casts serious doubt on any ground for abortion, apart from serious risk to the mother's life.

Other life-and-death issues cry out for investigation. What should our attitude be, for example, to suicide and mercy killing? Alas, I have run out of space! But the ground rules have been laid.

The taking of human life is always bad. If we ever do it, we shall be called to account by our Creator, in whose image every human being is made. But sometimes killing may be right, as the least evil of all the options available.

We cannot and must not opt out of making those lesser-evil choices. It is no good sheltering behind the smoke screen of God's sovereignty. He is Lord and Master of all human life, but he has delegated to men and women the task of managing it. The responsibilities involved are fearsome, but we dare not duck out of them.

TO THINK AND TALK ABOUT

1. Would you have voted with or against the majority of the medical students the author mentions at the start of this chapter? Why?

2. How does your answer to question 1 compare with the author's arguments for the value of human life? Do you want to modify your opinion in the light of what he says?

3. "You can do something *bad*—and be *right* to

do it," says the author. Do you agree that this "lesser-evil" approach is "the only biblical way out of many a moral dilemma"?

4. Do you think the author "asks the right questions" in his discussion of capital punishment?

5. How can the lesser-evil principle guide us as we think about war?

6. A friend, distressed to find she is pregnant, tells you she is trying to decide whether to have an abortion. How would you, as a Christian, counsel and support her? (You could tackle this as a role-play.)

7. There was no space in this chapter to investigate other life-and-death issues—but how would you apply the sixth commandment to (a) suicide and (b) euthanasia (bearing in mind the lesser-evil principle)?

NINE
Sex Is Good and Marriage Is Special: The Seventh Commandment

You shall not commit adultery.
(Exodus 20:14)

"The human body," wrote D. H. Lawrence, "is only just coming to real life. With the Greeks it gave a lovely flicker, then Plato and Aristotle killed it, and Jesus finished it off. But now, the body is coming really to life!"

Lady Chatterly certainly swallowed this philosophy of sexual liberation whole. So have many others since. And, as Lawrence suggests, it is Christianity that is branded as the repressive culprit.

THE GOODNESS OF SEX

Ask any ordinary person what he or she thinks the church's attitude toward sex is all about, and the chances are that the answer will have a negative ring to it. "You shall not commit adultery" implies, to many people, that Christianity looks down its religious nose at *all* sexual activity.

Unfortunately, a study of church history helps to bear that out. The great Augustine believed that Adam and Eve never had sexual intercourse in the Garden of Eden, in their perfect state. If they had, he added, it would have been a cool, controlled affair, unruffled by any emotional passion.

Even marriage came under the hammer. The leaders of the early church stopped short of labeling sex in marriage as sinful, but they certainly reckoned that it was better to stay celibate if you possibly could. Gregory of Nyssa described the married state as a "sad tragedy"; and Tertullian declared that the difference between sex inside and outside marriage was really only a matter of legal small print because the same "act of shame" lay behind both.

It is bewildering to find such negative statements from church leaders because, as we shall see, they contrast so sharply with the approach to sex we find in the Bible. What has happened?

Reading between the lines in the history books, it seems that a powerful antisex lobby had staged a successful takeover bid for Christian opinion. These heretics (because that is

what they were) taught that the body was infe-
rior to the mind and spirit. Sex, as a physical
function, should therefore be swept under life's
carpet, where it belonged with all the other dirt.

The Bible speaks about the human body with
a completely different voice. Indeed, the body
holds center stage throughout the New Testament. The gospel story begins by highlighting
the Incarnation (which means "in-*body*-ing") of
God's Son. And it ends by describing both the
crucifixion of Jesus, when "he himself bore our
sins in his body on the tree" (1 Peter 2:24), and
his resurrection, when he was at pains to show
his disciples that he was a risen *body,* not a ghost
(Luke 24:36-43).

In his letters, Paul is anxious to stop his Christian friends from thinking of themselves as
merely souls with legs. What they do with their
bodies, he insists, is as vital as their prayer discipline. Bodies are meant "for the Lord." They are
"members of Christ himself" and temples "of
the Holy Spirit." And naturally these facts color
the Christian's attitude toward his or her sexual
drive, because "he who sins sexually sins
against his own body" (1 Corinthians 6:13, 15,
18-19).

So back we come to sex. And, with the New
Testament's strong affirmation of body life in
the background, it comes as no surprise to find

that the biblical attitude toward sex is over-whelmingly positive. "May you rejoice in the wife of your youth," declares the book of Prov-erbs. "May her breasts satisfy you always, may you ever be captivated by her love" (5:18-19).

The Song of Songs is a book of the Bible that absolutely vibrates with delight in physical love-making. "Your eyes," croons the man, "are doves behind your veil. . . . Your lips are like a scarlet thread and your mouth is lovely. . . . You are all fair, my love; there is no fault in you. . . . You have ravished my heart with a glance of your eyes." And she is in the same throbbing ecstasy over him. "My lover is handsome and strong. . . . I belong to my lover, and he desires me. . . . My lover is mine, and I am his. . . . I am sick with love."

In New Testament times, Paul met young Christians from big towns such as Corinth and Ephesus who had major problems in their sex lives. Sexual vice was rampant. Many were so sickened by the kind of things they saw going on around every street corner (and, in many cases, in their own past as well) that they wanted noth-ing more to do with sex at all. Some began to preach an antisex message in the name of Christ.

That was the point where Paul felt he had to step in with a firm rebuke. Such men "forbid people to marry," he warned his young assistant

Timothy, who was then working in Ephesus in the shadow of Aphrodite's great temple of sex. They are wrong, because "everything God created is good." It was God, not the devil, who started sex off in the first place. So, like the rest of the Lord's good gifts, it is to be "received with thanksgiving" (1 Timothy 4:3-4).

Here is the essential background to the seventh commandment. Whatever else it is telling us, it is not casting sour looks at sex in itself. The whole Bible says a big, joyful yes! to human sexuality.

THE GOODNESS OF MARRIAGE

The commandment's purpose is, in fact, to set up a protective fence around sex in marriage. And, in filling that very positive role, it slaps a stern veto on all extramarital sexual intercourse.

We need to be absolutely clear at this point. The Bible's line on adultery is like society's approach to glue sniffing. Glue is great, but only for sticking things together. Use it to give yourself an artificial "high," and you are abusing it. Sex is meant for sticking people together in the tight bond of marriage. Applied in that way, it is great. But having sex outside marriage is using a good thing in the wrong way. So adultery, according to Scripture, is the sexual equivalent of solvent abuse.

This, of course, is the point where many people shake their heads and smile as if to say, "We told you so." Calling a halt to sex outside marriage seems an unnecessary restriction on an enjoyable experience. Providing they act responsibly to prevent unwanted pregnancies and sexually transmitted diseases, there is surely no point in stopping people from making love, whether they are married to their partners or not.

The Bible begs to differ. It is far less cynical about marriage than we are. It elevates wedlock to a place where it stands entirely distinct from every other human relationship. And it is because marriage is so special that adultery is so wrong. In the New Testament's words, "the marriage bed" should be "kept pure" because "marriage should be honored by all." That, and that alone, is why "God will judge the adulterer and all the sexually immoral" (Hebrews 13:4).

The special nature of marriage is rooted in a very special biblical idea. Above everything else, marriage is a *covenant.*

Covenants are binding agreements. And the most special covenant of them all, according to the Bible, is the loving agreement God made with his people.

Time after time, both the Old Testament and the New draw parallels between God's unique covenant with his people and the agreement a man and a woman make with each other when they get married. "I saw that the time had come for you to fall in love," the Lord reminds Israel. "I covered your naked body with my coat and promised to love you. Yes, I made a marriage covenant with you, and you became mine" (Ezekiel 16:8, TEV). "Husbands, love your wives, just as Christ loved the church and gave himself up for her," echoes Paul (Ephesians 5:25).

God's love for his people is like a marriage. And Christian married couples should model their relationships on the Lord's love for his bride, the church.

With that awesome comparison ringing in their ears, Christians are bound to think about marriage in a very special way. Those who become husbands and wives are making a covenant, just as God did. The consequences are well worth exploring.

Covenant and contract. In the first place, it means that marriage is more than a contract.

People enter into contracts when they want to buy and sell articles or services. There may be penalty clauses if the goods are not up to standard or if they are not delivered on time.

Marriage is bigger than that. Its focus is on giving, not bargaining. And the spotlight does not fall on the things the partners agree to provide for one another, but on the lives—and the selves—they promise to share. It is all part of what making a covenant involves.

To be fair, the Old Testament does not always read that way. Wives were bought, not wooed, in Bible times. Money figured prominently at the time of betrothal, when a sum was agreed upon as a guarantee against death or divorce. The bridegroom also paid an agreed amount to the bride's father to compensate him for the loss of an asset. And if a young wife was found to be substandard (not a virgin), or if she did not deliver the promised goods within ten years (in the shape of a baby), she could be sent packing.

In that sort of scenario, the status of women inevitably took a dive. Many wives (though by no means all) were undoubtedly treated as little more than baby-machines and household conveniences. But that kind of discriminating behavior does not really square with Old Testament teaching. Even the penal code distinguished between wives and property by making adultery a capital offense, while the maximum penalty for theft was just a fine. And the story of creation in Genesis, quoted by both Jesus and Paul as the foundation for marriage, describes a man and his wife as "one flesh" (Genesis 2:24).

That little phrase is, as we shall see, a particularly precious way of describing the depth of intimacy a married couple is meant to share. It lifts marriage high above the level of services provided and paid for. This is the language of covenant, not contract.

Covenant and children. Secondly, the marriage covenant is more than a license to start a family.

Many couples decide to get married once a baby is on the way. Living together without a marriage certificate is all right, they argue, as long as there are just the two of them. But children deserve the security of a more conventional home environment.

Their instinct is right, according to the Bible (at least in the second half of their reasoning). Families are the building blocks from which the whole community is constructed. Broken family relationships, as we saw in chapter 7, pose a direct threat to society. Schoolteachers, policemen, and social workers would all agree that lack of stability in the home breeds delinquents.

Getting married does not, of course, guarantee a stable family life. The latest figures for divorce are eloquent evidence of that. A marriage certificate cannot ensure a healthy home any more than a birth certificate can produce a healthy baby. But a certificate of birth does at least give a child's life a measure of protection. And the marriage certificate plays a similar role. Married fathers and mothers (however their marriages are recognized) may walk out on one another, but the piece of paper makes it a little harder for them to finish what they have officially started. They may even intend to escape their responsibilities for their children, but the divorce courts will have something to say if they try.

All this suggests that starting a family is a very good reason for getting married. But we must not turn that statement around and toughen up its wording. It is quite wrong to say that the *only* good reason for getting married is to start a family.

Once again, we are back to the idea of *covenant.* God instructed the first man and woman to "be fruitful and increase in number" (Genesis 1:28). But when he brought them together in their prototype marriage, the wording on the covenant read, "A man will leave his father and mother and be united to his wife, and they will become one flesh" (Genesis 2:24). There is no mention there of having babies. Covenant is all about a committed, united, "one flesh" relationship.

We can, in fact, bring the argument around in a full circle. The very best way of ensuring a stable family environment for the children is to cultivate a sound covenant relationship at the center.

My three grown-up children are not perfect,

as I hope they would agree. One reason is that they have far-from-perfect parents (and I know they would agree with that). But they do at least have a father and mother who really enjoy their "one flesh" unity. They have sometimes caught us having a quick cuddle in the kitchen. When that happens they poke fun at us unmercifully, but in their more serious moments they tell us never to be any different. In a curious way, they still find a little security in our covenanted togetherness.

Covenant and romance. In the third place, marriage is more than a romantic alliance.

Back in the swinging sixties, the American pop poet Rod McKuen came up with a new, off-beat version of the marriage ceremony. The setting he suggested is suitably romantic: a forest clearing. The sun is shining warmly (but not too hotly) through the leaves. The birds are singing their hearts out in the branches.

The couple take their vows. Each says to the other: "I believe in love. I believe the person I will walk away with today to start another lifetime with to be someone I wish to comfort, and I will expect comfort in return. I will share everything I have to share, and I will always expect the sharing and the giving to be returned."

The pastor then says his piece. "This is a vow

for forever. If forever should end for the two of you, or one of you, tomorrow, or next year, stay together only as long as you need each other. Go only when your need for the other ends."

That is a fascinating expression of the way many modern people in the romantic West view their sexual partnerships. Marriage (if you call it that) is a relationship between two consenting adults who continue in it so long as each finds it fulfilling. But once either or both falls out of love, the bond is broken.

Whatever the label you put on that kind of alliance, it is not a covenant.

For one thing, covenant *love* does not end when it is no longer returned. To illustrate that, we need to think back to the way God loves us. From God's perspective, we are not always very lovable. We must often seem downright hateful to him. We sometimes ignore him. Occasionally we may even return his love by throwing it back in his face. But his love for us never falters.

It is an awesomely high standard, but love within the marriage covenant should be just like that. Suppose you no longer find your wife physically attractive. Imagine (and it may not be too difficult) that your husband drives you right up the wall by his pigheaded insensitivity. Month follows month, and the two of you grow farther apart. Is your marriage dead?

No, it has not died. The romance may have gone out of the relationship, but covenant love can survive that kind of shock. The love that Jesus taught has its roots in the will, not the heart. It goes on deciding and acting in the other person's best interests, even when it has stopped feeling any affection. It carries on giving long after the getting has disappeared. It persists through disillusionment, through dislike—and even through hatred.

The New Testament, using covenant language, says, "Husbands, love your wives, just as Christ loved the church and gave himself up for her" (Ephesians 5:25). Think of your own church. Then put yourself in Jesus' place. If *he* can go on loving *that,* my last paragraph is more than a load of idealistic nonsense, isn't it?

For another thing, covenant *fidelity* does not end when its needs are no longer met. God says to his people, "I will betroth you to me forever" (Hosea 2:19). For Rod McKuen, "forever" can end tomorrow. But that is the language of romance, not covenant.

Once again, the Bible redirects us to God's example. If we want to know what fidelity in a relationship really means, we need look no further than the way God persisted and persevered with his people. Hosea's prophecy paints that picture in painfully dazzling colors. The prophet's own marriage was a disaster. His wife was repeatedly unfaithful. She left him for other men again and again, "just like my marriage to my people," God assured him. And the Lord illustrated his own divine determination to stick to his covenant commitment by insisting that Hosea take his wife back in spite of every provocation.

Covenant fidelity is totally committed. That is what distinguishes being married from cohabiting.

Covenant and cohabiting. More and more couples are deciding to live together without troubling the registrar for a marriage certificate. Their reasons for not marrying are varied and sometimes quite complex.

Some intend to marry eventually. They may be engaged, so why not anticipate the wedding day? Or, if one partner is already married, they may simply be waiting for the divorce paperwork to be completed. It may make good economic sense to live together in the meantime. Why pay rent for two apartments when one will do?

Others may be trying to decide whether marriage is right for them or not. The only way to find out, they reckon, is to experiment before taking the final legal step.

Others again want a relationship that is better than marriage. Some time ago I went away for a weekend with a group of Christian students. Our preset theme was "love and marriage." To start things off, I asked how many of them would seriously consider cohabiting as an alternative to marrying. To my surprise, the vast majority said they would. I was even more surprised when they gave me their reasons. Most of them had such negative experiences of marriage themselves (mainly from home) that they were convinced God must have something better in store for them than that.

Still others prefer to hang on to their freedom. They see the wedding bond as bondage. Cohabiting offers the sexual experience and emotional closeness of marriage, with the independence of staying single. That sounds like a good deal.

Whatever the reasons, nothing can disguise the fact that cohabiting is different from marriage because it lacks commitment to fidelity. Some unmarried couples may protest that they *feel* much more committed to one another than they would if they were man and wife. Because their partnership is not "safe," they take extra trouble to maintain it. But the truth is that (in a society that does not recognize common-law marriage) either of them can walk out of the relationship at the drop of a hat.

One of my students described the difference to me very vividly. He is married, but his sister is not—though she lives with her boyfriend. "If my sister broke up with her boyfriend," he told me, "my parents would welcome her back home without any questions. But if I tried to go home after a row with my wife, they would tell me to go back to her."

This is what makes "trial marriage" a nonstarter. People who get married are saying, "We are going into this for life." You cannot experiment with that kind of commitment in advance. It is something you either accept—and work at—or reject. The pledged fidelity of the marriage covenant defies any simulation.

If you do make that covenant commitment, it is true that you sacrifice your freedom to walk out of it. But wedlock is not a padlock. Commitment to lifelong fidelity actually enlarges a married couple's experience of freedom. Husband and wife can share personal intimacies in the liberated confidence that their secrets will go no farther. They can have genuinely safe sex, because they do not constantly need to make a big impression to forestall other liaisons. Close friends do not become competitors. Where there is genuine fidelity, there is no need to ask, "Why are you so late?" or, "What have you been doing with Tom [or Sarah] while I've been away?"

It is interesting to see how secular society is
catching up with the values of covenanted fidelity. A recent article in *Cosmopolitan* magazine
announced: "The once fashionable cry, 'I don't
want to commit myself,' is becoming markedly
less trendy." The author of the article inter-
viewed a woman of twenty, just married, who
had had "six years of supposed fun" after losing
her virginity at fourteen. "Many people reacted
with incredulity when I announced I was getting
married," she confessed. "They seemed to think
it tantamount to death, the end of freedom. But I
think that is reflective of our cynical age. I love
Tim and wanted to cement our relationship. The
security of marriage lured, and for me it tri-
umphed over the trifling—in comparison—bene-
fits of independence."

THE BADNESS OF ADULTERY

Adultery *is* bad. The seventh commandment
says that very bluntly. And the reason for its bad-
ness is simply because it breaks the marriage
covenant more blatantly than anything else a
husband or a wife can do. Their commitment to
fidelity has been betrayed.

This gives a very high profile to sexual intercourse. Too high, some may think. Marriage is
certainly bigger than sex. And many marriages

break down for reasons other than sexual unfaithfulness.

Becoming one flesh. True though that is, the Bible sets the sex act right at the heart of the meaning of marriage. Earlier on, we noticed the one-sentence description of marriage that Jesus picked up from the story of creation. It is worth repeating. "A man will leave his father and mother and be united to his wife, and they will become one flesh" (Genesis 2:24; see also Matthew 19:5). Becoming one flesh is the seal on the marriage covenant. And it means having sexual intercourse.

To be sure, it means more than that. We get the real sense of *flesh* in this context by dropping off the final *h* and spelling the rest of the word backwards. Becoming one flesh is more of a process than an event. It means the total giving of self on both sides of the partnership. It involves deeply shared thoughts and feelings, as well as joint accounts and a double bed. And that kind of thing does not happen overnight.

Nevertheless, sexual intercourse is a vital part of this amazing process of becoming totally intimate. Lying naked with someone you love is the most devastatingly appropriate physical expression of your desire to lay bare every thought and feeling you have ever had.

Think of intercourse as a kind of body language. We use lots of different physical gestures to signal our feelings. A warm handshake says, "I'm really pleased to meet you." A kiss and a cuddle say, "I like you a lot." Culture makes a difference, of course. Eskimos rub noses and Arabs embrace.

But what does sexual intercourse say? Well, here we have to jump a wide gap between the Bible's teaching and the views that dominate the media today. According to Scripture, intercourse is a unique kind of body language. It says, "Whatever the future holds, we give ourselves to each other for the rest of our lives; and the oneness we share will always remain exclusive to us."

This takes us right back to the marriage covenant, with its pledge of committed fidelity. Intercourse is appropriate body language for that very special kind of relationship. So the opposite must be true as well. As an expression of any *other* kind of relationship, sexual intercourse is grossly *in*appropriate.

In Corinth, Paul met people (inside the church) who tried to tell him that sex was just an appetite. Two people are hungry, so they sit down to a good meal. They are sexually aroused, so they lie down for a night of pleasant relief (1 Corinthians 6:13).

Paul resisted that line of thinking with every fiber of his Christian being. Do those people not know what sexual intercourse is really saying? Have they not understood what the Bible means about "becoming one flesh" (verse 16)?

Having sexual intercourse outside marriage is telling a lie. It is saying something with your body that you do not mean. So you honestly fancy one another, do you? So you are wearing a condom? So what? What you are doing adds up to a sin against your body (verse 18). And remember, if you are a Christian, you are talking about the body God the Father made for himself, the body God the Son bought by his blood, and the body God the Holy Spirit uses as his home (verses 13, 15, 19-20).

Dimensions of adultery. During this chapter, I have been talking about adultery and extramarital intercourse as though they are the same thing. That is true, I believe, to the Bible's teaching as a whole. But it is not quite fair to the cultural context in which the seventh commandment itself is set.

In Old Testament times, adultery meant something quite narrow and specific. The spotlight fell on the woman, not the man. A wife committed adultery when she had intercourse with any man except her husband. But the same standard did not apply to him. If he had sex with another *married* woman, he was guilty of adultery (against the woman's husband). He was not considered an adulterer, however, if he went to bed with a prostitute or a single girl.

This piece of sexual discrimination was almost certainly due to the high profile Israelite society gave to keeping the family bloodlines pure. With Christ's arrival, that particular need was no longer the top priority. So it comes as no surprise to find the definition of adultery expanded in the New Testament.

Jesus broadened his followers' understanding of adultery in two important ways. They found both of them very hard to accept.

In the first place, *he condemned mental adultery.* The root of sexual unfaithfulness, he insisted, is to be found in the heart, not the genitals (Matthew 15:19). No man can pat himself on the back for avoiding an affair if he has secretly taken the pretty girl next door to bed in his vivid imagination (Matthew 5:27-28).

Jesus was not, of course, saying it is wrong to be tempted. After all, he was himself "tempted in every way, just as we are." But he never sinned (Hebrews 4:15). There is all the difference in the world between being tempted to sin sexually and yielding to the pressure.

Nevertheless, temptation and sin are on the

same track. The wise Christian will take great pains to make sure the one does not become the other. The Bible is very practical about that. "I made a covenant with my eyes," said Job, "not to look lustfully at a girl" (Job 31:1). Reading soft porn or switching on a late-night TV movie are not the best ways of insuring against committing adultery in the mind.

Secondly, *Jesus condemned divorce and remarriage as adultery.* "Anyone who divorces his wife and marries another woman commits adultery against her," he told his followers. "And if she divorces her husband and marries another man, she commits adultery" (Mark 10:11-12). That made the disciples gasp, "If this is the situation between a husband and wife, it is better not to marry" (Matthew 19:10).

They were not only worried by Jesus' insistence that marriage vows could not be set aside. In a couple of sentences, he had smashed to pieces the Jewish male's traditional position of privilege. As far as Jesus was concerned, husbands and wives were completely on the same level when their marriages broke down.

But this was not quite Jesus' last word on divorce. Matthew's Gospel has a slightly expanded version of his teaching. When the marriage covenant has been breached by sexual unfaithfulness, he taught, both divorce and remarriage may be justified (Matthew 5:32; 19:9).

Was that doublethink on Jesus' part? It certainly sounds rather like it. Or had Matthew misunderstood the strictness of the Lord's line on remarriage and wrongly watered it down by introducing an exception?

I find both those alternatives unconvincing. We have here, I believe, the Bible's most striking example of the lesser-evil principle at work. In chapter 8, I suggested that this principle is the key to understanding the Bible's teaching on killing. Now we hear Jesus measuring marriage by the same ethical criterion.

What he is saying (if I have understood him correctly) is that divorce is always *bad*. But just sometimes, as the least bad of all the available options, it may be *right*. Moses had followed exactly the same principle when he introduced his "certificate of divorce" in Old Testament times (see Deuteronomy 24:1-4). And so did Paul, when he later struggled with the kind of "mixed marriage" situation in Corinth that Jesus never had to face in Judea (see 1 Corinthians 7:10-15).

This "solution" is far less tidy than a total ban on divorce. But it does bring into play other important biblical principles, like forgiveness and the possibility of a new start. And it need not open the floodgates to easy remarriage.

As Joy Davidman rightly says, serial marriages are really nothing more than attacks of chronic adultery. There is absolutely no encouragement in Scripture for anything of that sort. Moses' bill of divorce contained built-in deterrents to marriage breakdown. Jesus made it clear that only the most serious breach of the marriage covenant could make divorce even thinkable. And Paul advised Christian partners in spiritually mixed marriages to stay with their partners right up to the point of final desertion. The Bible's exceptions are last resorts, not let-out clauses.

Finally, it is worth noticing that *the New Testament brackets homosexual intercourse with adultery.* In his first letter to Timothy, Paul includes an updated version of the Ten Commandments. The parallel to the seventh commandment is particularly explicit. God's law condemns "adulterers *and perverts,"* he writes (1 Timothy 1:10).

Paul's word for "pervert" is really two words rolled into one. It is the word for "intercourse" added to the word for "male." The message is clear enough. A man who has sexual intercourse with another man has done the equivalent of committing adultery.

Paul is even more detailed in his letter to the

Romans. Practicing homosexuals, including lesbians, have "exchanged natural relations for unnatural ones," he writes (Romans 1:26-27). They may *feel* they are acting naturally when they have physical intercourse, but they are in fact using their sexual organs in an unnatural way. God's creation plan for human sexuality is to bring together Adams and Eves, not members of the same sex.

There is, of course, far more to say about such vexed issues as divorce and homosexuality than that. The Ten Commandments only give us the headlines. But God's caption over human sexuality could not be more clear. Adultery is bad, not because sexual intercourse is morally dubious, but because marriage is so precious. Intercourse is meant to seal a relationship between a man and a woman that is exclusive and lifelong. To make it say anything else is to turn it into a lie.

TO THINK AND TALK ABOUT

1. "The Bible is antisex." How would you answer a friend who expressed this belief?

2. Three common ideas of marriage today are: (a) a contract; (b) an arrangement to enter into when a baby is on the way; (c) a romantic alliance. What makes the Bible's concept of marriage as *covenant* much richer than any of

these? (Married and engaged couples: Why not make a point of discussing your own idea of marriage and seeing how it measures up to the Bible's teaching?)

3. Which couple do you think is more truly free: a couple who live together or the couple who are "covenant-married"? Why?

4. What does "becoming one flesh" mean? Do you agree with the author that sex outside marriage is like "telling a lie"?

5. How did Jesus broaden his followers' understanding of adultery? How far do you agree with the author's conclusions on divorce?

6. A Christian friend confesses to feeling attracted to members of the same sex. How would you talk this through with him or her?

TEN
Not Owners But Caretakers: The Eighth Commandment

You shall not steal. (Exodus 20:15)

At the college where I work, we know all about stealing. That is because we live in an affluent area of north London that attracts burglaries as surely as light attracts moths. The college's outside doors bristle with security devices, but the thieves still get in from time to time. Secretaries' handbags vanish during the lunch hour. Students' checkbooks disappear from their studies.

Our reaction to thieves is a mixture of resentment and hostility. How dare they lay their grubby hands on our hard-earned property?

One evening, a pile of top-quality bricks stood stacked at the end of the college drive, ready for use in extending a wall. Three young men arrived and began loading the bricks into a builder's van. Someone challenged them. She was greeted by a stream of abuse, so she concluded (quite rightly) that they were stealing the bricks. She phoned the police and in the meantime a student blocked the van's escape route with his car. More students and staff arrived on the scene, easily outnumbering the intruders.

The police did not arrive for half an hour. In the meantime two things happened. Two of the men unloaded the bricks from the van and returned them to the original stack. And while that was going on, the third member of the gang confronted those who barred his escape.

He had a way with words and a passing knowledge of theology. With the language adjusted, the one-way conversation went something like this.

"Call yourselves Christians, do you? I thought you were meant to forgive and turn the other cheek. Why are you handing us over to the police, then? And why are you fussing over a few bricks? We need them more than you do. Our little firm is going bust, but your place looks OK to me. Where's your Christian love? Isn't generosity a Christian virtue? You ought to *give* us the bricks!"

He was met with tight lips, but one or two pairs of feet shuffled awkwardly. The truth is that, as colleges go, Oak Hill is relatively well-off. We do not have to survive on income from students' fees alone. With admirable foresight, our founder endowed a trust that is efficiently managed by a group of dedicated trustees. We never have enough to do everything we want (who does?), but the trust's annual income subsidizes our work to a considerable extent. It also helps to maintain the college's physical environment. That consists of nearly sixty acres of park land, an amenity enjoyed by fewer than three hundred people at the northern edge of a crowded capital city.

We are immensely grateful for all these resources. But they do raise a few uncomfortable questions. We live on investment income. But when does investment become speculation, and when does speculation turn into "institutional theft" through the victimization of the weak by the powerful? The thought of victimizing anybody is miles away from our trustees' intentions, but *if* that is the bottom of the slippery slope that yields our income at the top, ought we not to be concerned?

Again, it is written into our trust deed that all funds must be applied to the college (and to the school that the trust also supports). We could not express our love and generosity by giving our bricks away, even if we managed to find a worthier cause than a firm of cowboy builders. If generosity is the other side of the coin to theft, as Paul suggests (in Ephesians 4:28), how—as an institution—can we express it?

And what about our lovely environment? We fence it off to keep vandals out, but are we not thereby robbing our more crowded neighbors of a precious amenity?

Questions like these may seem far removed from picking pockets or shoplifting. They are, in fact, very close indeed to the spirit of the eighth commandment. In its Old Testament setting, the main aim of this commandment was not to protect the wealthy from predators. Its primary purpose was to stop the rich from exploiting the poor.

PROPERTY AND POSSESSIONS

First, though, an even more radical question calls for a good answer. Is it not unchristian to own *anything*?

"You shall not steal" is a commandment with a hidden agenda. It suggests that God smiles on private possessions. It implies that Proudhon, the nineteenth-century Marxist, was misguided when he exclaimed, "Property is theft." If it is wrong for me to steal your property, it cannot be wrong for you to have it.

But did not Jesus, in his warnings about wealth, fire a torpedo beneath the waterline of the eighth commandment by questioning the morality of owning anything at all?

Jesus and poverty. The four Gospels certainly give personal wealth a bad press. "How hard it is for the rich to enter the kingdom of God!" warned Jesus (Mark 10:23). Affluence, he taught, can destroy our peace (Matthew 6:24-34), blind us to the needs of others (Luke 16:19-31), stand between us and the gateway to eternal life (Mark 10:17-27), and even bring down God's judgment on our heads (Luke 12:16-21). He told his disciples not to accumulate personal wealth (Matthew 6:19), and he praised those who gave up their possessions (Matthew 19:29).

It was Jesus' command to the rich young man, "Sell everything you have," that launched Francis of Assisi on his ministry. In his biography of Francis, G. K. Chesterton contrasts the unhappiness of the man in the Gospels who found this command too much for him, with the great joy Francis experienced as he took the Lord at his word: "He went out half-naked into the winter woods, walking the frozen ground beneath frosty trees; a man without a father. He was penniless, he was parentless, he was to all appearance without a trade or a plan or a hope in the world; and as he went under the frosty trees, he burst suddenly into song."

Attitudes to possessions. Francis, no doubt, saw
much in his own self-imposed poverty that
matched the example of Jesus who "though he
was rich, yet for your sakes he became poor"
(2 Corinthians 8:9). And yet the allusion to
Jesus' meeting with the rich young man should
make us pause, however vivid and formative
that incident became for Francis centuries later.
As far as we know, Jesus never said, "Sell everything you have" to anyone else. This was special
medicine for a special case, not a general prescription for all Christians to take. That young
man's problem did not lie in his wealth, but in
his attitude toward it. He had allowed his possessions to possess him.

This message echoes loudly and clearly
through another New Testament passage that is
often misunderstood. In his account of the Christian church's first few months of life, Luke tells
us how "all the believers were together and had
everything in common. Selling their possessions
and goods, they gave to anyone as he had need"
(Acts 2:44-45). Such generosity is breathtaking,
but it did not anticipate communist theory or
spring from a negative attitude toward private
ownership. As Christian gave to Christian, property changed hands. It did not suddenly become
public instead of private (even when the apostles
acted as a clearing house—see Acts 4:34-35).

One person's possessions simply became another's as a response to human need.

There was no compulsion about it either. The moral failure that led soon afterward to the frightening deaths of Ananias and Sapphira was deceit, not refusal to give. After selling some property, this couple pretended to give all the proceeds away, while secretly squirreling some of the cash for themselves. "Didn't it belong to you before it was sold?" asked Peter. "And after it was sold, wasn't the money at your disposal?" (Acts 5:4).

It is attitudes that count. This is the Bible's simple but searching contribution to the debate about possessing things.

Depending on God. The Old Testament patriarchs became very rich men, but their dependence on God did not waver, and it was this humble attitude to their Provider that made them morally healthy as well as materially wealthy. As Abraham's servant put it, "The LORD has blessed my master abundantly, and he has become wealthy" (Genesis 24:35). The same could not be said for Achan, one of Abraham's later descendants. His attempt to get rich quick by disobeying God's direct orders brought him terminal trouble, not material blessing (Joshua 7).

Depending on God is a risky business, as far

as material comforts are concerned. That is a dimension of the Bible's teaching on health and wealth that is sometimes missing from modern books on the subject. God certainly entrusts rich resources to some people who depend on him. But he also leads others into situations where they barely survive.

Once again, attitudes are the key. Job got it right when he reacted to disaster with worship: "The LORD gave and the LORD has taken away; may the name of the LORD be praised" (Job 1:21). And Paul displayed the same awesomely practical trust in God when he wrote from his prison cell: "I know what it is to be in need, and I know what it is to have plenty. I have learned the secret of being content in any and every situation. . . . I can do everything through him who gives me strength" (Philippians 4:12-13; compare 1 Timothy 6:6-8).

Not owners but caretakers. The eighth commandment certainly protects our right to have and keep things. But the Bible as a whole defines that right very carefully. It roots it firmly in responsibility. From a Christian point of view, I do not *own* anything at all—if by "owning" something I mean having the right to use and dispose of it just as I like. I am not so much an owner as a caretaker.

Responsibility and trust. The school caretaker who acts as though he owns the property under his care is not likely to keep his job for long. If he decides to sell "his" games equipment and lock the teaching staff out of "his" physics laboratory, he is abusing the position of responsibility he has been given.

The Bible sets human ownership in a similar framework. It is not pious nonsense but biblical principle that reminds me to look through a caretaker's eyes at everything I possess. I do not *own* either my car or my toothbrush. True, I have bought both with "my" money, but I do not really own that either. My wage, together with the talents and energy I use to earn it, have been given to me in trust. I am responsible to my divine Owner for the way I use and conserve anything and everything I have. If I am honest, I do not always think about things that way. But, as a Christian, I should.

And even that is not quite the end of the biblical story. According to the New Testament, God does not simply own my possessions. He owns *me*. Paul uses the language of the slave market to drive that point home. "You are not your own," he insists; "you were bought at a price" (1 Corinthians 6:19 20). So I am not just the caretaker of God's property. I am the trustee of a human life, which belongs to him although I call it my own.

Here is a farther blow struck against the idea of ownership. We tend to value people by the quantity and quality of what they possess. Instinctively, we show more respect for the business tycoon in his gleaming Rolls Royce than we do for the newspaper boy on his secondhand bike. We may even think that God does the same, smiling more broadly on the man who has "made it," in much the same way as a bank manager favors the clients with the biggest credit balances. Nothing, of course, could be further from the truth. God has paid for the lives of tramps and tycoons with the same currency—the blood of Jesus. Any two people have the same value to him, however much or however little they possess, because he owns them as well as their property.

Responsibility and care. The "caretaker" mentality is the antidote to materialism. If I take my responsibility to God seriously, I will conserve what he has given me and I will use it wisely. Globally, that will make me speak out against waste. I will protest against the unfair distribution of precious resources that makes the rich richer and the poor poorer. And at the personal level, I will resist the advertiser's pressure to buy things that I do not need, with money that could be given away to those worse off than I am.

I will trust God, too, to meet my needs (though not always my wants). That is much harder. Giving away an excess is far, far easier than depending on God in a crisis.

If we are to appreciate the full meaning of the eighth commandment, this is the background against which we must see it. In the Bible's eyes, stealing is bad caretaking. Whether I take something that belongs to somebody else, or keep things that are designed for distribution to other people, I am abusing the responsibility that God has given me as his trustee.

TAKING THINGS

It is amazing how many ways we find to justify stealing.

I think of someone I know who works in an office. He puts in many hours of overtime but is not paid any extra for his efforts. So, he says to himself, "Why not stick a few of the firm's stamps on my letters and use the office cellophane tape to wrap my Christmas parcels? It's one way of putting a wrong to rights, after all. And anyway, the firm is big enough to absorb such a tiny loss without noticing."

Shoplifting is only a step away from that.

Those faceless tycoons who own the supermarket down the road will not miss anything, as they laze away their days on the Costa Geriatrica, I reckon, if I pocket a bag of sweets from the confectionery shelf. If they knew I was out of work and my kids had no pocket money, they would probably give me the sweets anyway. And even if they wouldn't, they should.

Did someone say "faceless"? Life these days is managed by anonymous corporations and consortiums. They're all crooks, I tell myself, and the biggest crook of all is the government—whatever the color of its politics. Life is a continual struggle between us and "them out there." I wouldn't dream of taking a coin from my mother's purse, but dodging a fare or concealing a good little earner from the tax auditor is not really stealing, is it? Everybody does it who has the guts to try.

I hope you are not convinced! For one thing, arguments like these just do not make sense.

Respecting the law. Basically, they are selfish. Small thefts add up to huge losses. It is the petty thieves and shoplifters who increase the prices in the supermarkets and on the buses. They may be clever enough to get away with it themselves, but it is their friends and relations who pay for the hidden surcharges and the sophisticated surveillance systems that result. And the logical end of selfishness is anarchy.

We have a most unpopular tax in the United Kingdom at the moment (though it is in the process of being replaced). There are a few people who like the "community charge," as the government prefers to call it, because they benefit from the changes it has brought; but the majority find themselves much worse off. Some cannot pay the tax without suffering a severe cut in their basic living standards. Can't Pay, Won't Pay is a slogan to be seen in apartment windows as well as on noisy marches.

In a democratic society, the authorities cannot stay deaf to a popular outcry. But if every individual felt it right to stop paying a tax that he or she believed to be unjust, the democratic process itself would fall to pieces. Our schools would close and the refuse would pile up in our streets.

There are very few states of affairs worse than anarchy. That conviction lay behind Paul's instruction to Christians living under a harsh, totalitarian regime at Rome. "It is necessary to submit to the authorities, not only because of possible punishment but also because of conscience," he wrote. "This is also why you pay taxes, for the authorities are God's servants" (Romans 13:5-6).

Abusing the law. The end does not justify the means. But this is not to say that a bad law should not be challenged. Indeed, the law (and the authorities behind the law) may actually connive at theft.

That certainly happened in Bible times. And when it did, God's spokesmen did not remain silent. Jezebel manipulated the process of law to help her husband, King Ahab, get his hands on a poor neighbor's vineyard. "You have sold yourself to do evil in the eyes of the LORD," the prophet Elijah warned him bluntly (1 Kings 21:20). "Woe to those who make unjust laws," echoed Isaiah, "to those who issue oppressive decrees, to deprive the poor of their rights and rob my oppressed people of justice" (Isaiah 10:1-2).

In Jesus' day, the law-backed taxation system was widely abused. The occupying Roman authorities farmed out the collection of taxes to local men and turned a blind eye to the way they raised the revenue. It comes as no surprise to find tax collectors bracketed with "sinners" in Jewish eyes, because they often used their financial muscle to extort more money than was due to them. So when Zacchaeus, the tax man of Jericho, became a disciple of Jesus, one practical sign of his changed life-style was the reimbursement of his victims—with 400 percent interest (Luke 19:8).

The scope of the eighth commandment is, therefore, remarkably wide. It convicts the tax inspector as well as the tax dodger, and the political leader just as much as the unemployed man who steals to pay his rent. Not all thieves come at night with stockings over their faces. Some operate in broad daylight, dressed in smart business suits, defrauding their workers and their customers by late payment and inflated price-fixing (see Leviticus 19:13; Hosea 12:7; and Amos 8:5).

DISTRIBUTING THINGS FAIRLY

Stealing is an abuse of caretaking. It often involves *taking* something that has been entrusted to the care of someone else. But it may also take on a slightly different shape. God asks his caretakers to distribute his resources fairly. So (as the Bible sees it) stealing can mean *keeping* something that should really be given away to others.

Responsibility and power. Once again, the spotlight falls on attitudes. Owners derive power from their possessions. The more they have, the more powerful they become. And the more powerful they become, the more things they are able to add to their personal collection. So the rich get richer and the poor get poorer. As Ronald

Wallace points out, wealth flows up as surely as water flows down.

Caretakers, on the other hand, have responsibilities. The more they look after, the greater is their responsibility to use "their" things as the owner wishes. And Christians spell *owner* with a capital *O*.

It is when the focus shifts from responsibility to power that caretaking takes on the appearance of ownership. And once that happens, abuse is only just around the corner.

The lawmakers and prophets of Old Testament times pinpointed this peril very clearly. The well-known Old Testament veto on usury was not meant as an attack on profit making as such. It was aimed at abuse of power. The moneylender's temptation was to turn his clients into victims. He turned others' misfortunes into his own profit, as he tightened the financial screw ever more and more relentlessly. The unfortunate borrower could finish up minus money, property, family—and even personal liberty.

When the rich and powerful become indifferent to the plight of the poor and weak, they are bad caretakers. And the divine Owner is not pleased. "Do not take advantage of a widow or an orphan," he warns them. "If you do and they cry out to me, I will certainly hear their cry" (Exodus 22:22-23). Exploitation is a form of theft. That is why Jesus acted so vigorously against the businessmen who took advantage of worshipers in the temple at Jerusalem by pushing up the exchange rate and inflating the price of doves. He accused them of turning God's house into a "den of robbers" (Mark 11:15-17).

It is not hard to find modern parallels. British clearing banks regularly break the spirit of the eighth commandment in the way they deal with young people. Nineteen-year-olds are allowed to run up huge debit balances on their current accounts. When they are unable to cover their debt, a loan is offered at a high rate of interest. And when they fall behind with the repayments on that, they are taken to court. I know one young man who left home in fear and desperation when he was faced with a court order, and another who was still receiving offers of more loans from the same bank months after his debt had been paid off by a third party.

Centuries ago, Thomas Watson, the Puritan writer, commented on the eighth commandment by condemning the usurer who "seems to help another by letting him have money in his necessity, but gets him into bonds, and sucks out his very blood and marrow." Driving a hard bargain when the other person's need is great adds up to stealing, according to the Bible. Put another way, it is appallingly bad caretaking to add to a surplus while others are in grave need (see Isaiah 5:8). If the Old Testament prophets were let loose today, they would surely be far more concerned with the exploitation of the developing world's resources than with pickpocketing in expensive restaurants (see Isaiah 3:15; Amos 8:4-7).

Responsibility and generosity. God wants his caretakers to be generous. In the New Testament, Paul takes up that prominent biblical theme and applies it directly to stealing: "He who has been stealing must steal no longer, but must work, doing something useful with his own hands, that he may have something to share with those in need" (Ephesians 4:28).

One of our former students tells a remarkable story. One night, she and her husband slept through a would-be burglary. When they got up, they found a five-pound note on the kitchen table. On top of it was another note, written by the thief. It read, "As your need is greater than mine, you had better have this." They checked carefully, but nothing had been taken.

Their nighttime visitor with the sense of humor had not quite captured the spirit of Paul's instruction (presumably he went on to burgle my friends' wealthier neighbors). But he was getting quite close to it. Generosity is the antidote to theft. In the psalmist's words, "The wicked borrow and do not repay, but the righteous give generously" (Psalm 37:21). Or, as a modern philanthropist put it, "Wealth is power—power to do good." Christian caretakers cooperate to meet each others' needs. They do not act like quasi-owners, competing to get their hands on each others' possessions.

And in behaving that way, they are simply following in their Owner's footsteps. "For you know the grace of our Lord Jesus Christ, that though he was rich, yet for your sakes he became poor, so that you through his poverty might become rich" (2 Corinthians 8:9).

So, the eighth commandment has unexpectedly wide horizons. It asks uncomfortable questions about our attitudes to possessions— whether "ours" or other people's. We are called to be caretakers, not owners. And that means we are as guilty of theft when we fail to distribute God's resources generously as we are when we seize them for ourselves unjustly.

TO THINK AND TALK ABOUT

1. Presumably you're not in the habit of robbing banks or picking pockets. Does this mean that you don't need to think about how this commandment might apply to you?

2. "Property is theft" (Proudhon). Would Jesus have agreed?

3. "I am not so much an owner as a caretaker." What are some implications of this biblical attitude to property?

4. Many "ordinary, decent" people take or use what belongs to someone else without ever thinking of it as stealing. What forms can it take? Can it ever be right?

5. The author applies this commandment to those who use their power to exploit others. How does this challenge (a) our personal lives, (b) our business lives, and (c) government policies in areas such as taxation and overseas aid?

6. What are some practical ways in which we can use our money and possessions in a way that follows our Owner's example?

ELEVEN
Words That Damage: The Ninth Commandment

You shall not give false testimony against your neighbor. (Exodus 20:16)

It was a stupid thing to do. After buying a toy gun, Mike had used it to rob a lady in a sweet shop. He only got a few pounds. And he was caught.

The lady was in her seventies, so Mike might easily have found himself on a murder charge. As it was, he was remanded on bail by the local magistrates. I got to know him while he was waiting for his trial. He came to a Bible study group that happened to be meeting in the house next door to his. The story of Jesus hit him hard. The fact that God's Son had died to save him from his sins was great news for Mike, and it was not long before he became a Christian.

So it was that a month or two later I found

myself facing a judge, resplendent in his wig
and robes. Unlike Mike, I was not on trial, but
the occasion was awesome enough without any
extra complications like that. I was there to
speak up for Mike as a character witness. My
job was to persuade the judge—if I could—that,
since his conversion, Mike was a changed man.
Could I do it? Could I find the words to convince the court that the accused (who had
pleaded guilty) would not offend again? And did
I completely believe that myself?

The questions raced around my mind as I
waited. Was Mike's "conversion" just a ploy to
escape punishment? If I painted too glowing a
picture of his reformed Christian character,
would I be telling the truth, the whole truth, and
nothing but the truth?

In a word, was I in danger of breaking the
ninth commandment?

Not literally, perhaps. The commandment
says, "You shall not give false testimony *against*
your neighbor." I was speaking for Mike, not
against him. And the procedure at the Winches-
ter Quarter Assizes, with solicitors and barristers
facing each other across the well of the court,
was rather more complex than the way justice
was dispensed at the gate of an Israelite village.

Nevertheless, the power of words was never
more real. The scope for twisting the truth could

hardly be greater than in a Western court of law. The prosecution counsel bends his eloquence to secure a conviction, whether or not the defendant is guilty. The defense fights for words to get the accused man acquitted, whether or not he is innocent. And all the people who are cross-examined in the witness box, from the arresting officer right through to the character reference, speak to their own hidden agendas. In the middle of it all, the truth either emerges or stays hidden.

The ninth commandment is all about *truth* and the power of *words*. Both, according to the Bible, are desperately important.

THE POWER OF THE TONGUE

"Let's attack him with our tongues," plotted Jeremiah's enemies (Jeremiah 18:18). It was no idle threat, as Jeremiah soon found out. Words make powerful weapons. As the book of Proverbs neatly puts it, "Like a club or a sword or a sharp arrow is the man who gives false testimony against his neighbor" (Proverbs 25:18).

James's brief letter in the New Testament underlines this truth very vividly. James often dipped his pen in poster paint to make his point, and in chapter 3 of his letter, he draws several dramatic pictures of the tongue at work.

"The tongue is a small part of the body," he

writes, "but it makes great boasts." Its influence
is out of all proportion to its size, like the bit in a
horse's mouth or the rudder that alters the course
of a transatlantic liner. "Consider what a great
forest is set on fire by a small spark," James
comments. Leave a smoldering cigarette stub in
dry grass after a picnic, and the effect can be
devastating.

Bits, rudders, and sparks are, of course, very
useful things in themselves. So is the tongue.
The world's problems would not be solved by a
universal vow of silence, any more than a horse-
woman would prefer to ride without a bit in her
horse's mouth or a ship's captain steer without a
rudder.

But James wants to make a more serious
point. He has some more somber pictures for us
to look at. Words are like fire, coloring agents,
and drugs, he continues. They can be dreadfully
abused as well as marvelously used. As the fire
that warms the camper can burn down a hospital
hundreds of miles away if it is allowed to get out
of control, so the undisciplined tongue can "set
the whole course of life on fire." Using words
carelessly is like putting a red shirt in the wash-
ing machine with your whites; they "stain the
whole person." There is even a sinister quality
about the tongue, James concludes. Like a lethal

chemical agent, it is "full of deadly poison" (verses 6-8).

James's antidote is typically practical. The tongue must be used sparingly and carefully if its great power is not to be abused. "Everyone should be quick to listen, slow to speak and slow to become angry" (1:19). In motoring terms, the brake should be used twice as often as the accelerator—or, as a small card I picked up at a station newsstand puts it, "Make sure your brain is engaged before putting your mouth into gear." Motoring organizations advise drivers who are involved in accidents or caught in police traps not to say one word more than is strictly necessary. This is wise, James-like advice.

It expresses a Jesus-like approach to life, too. The more Jesus was provoked, the less he actually said. Toward the end of his life, he became a victim of those who broke the ninth commandment literally. In the court of the Sanhedrin, "many testified falsely against him," Mark reports. "Then the high priest stood up before them and asked Jesus, 'Are you not going to answer? What is this testimony that these men are bringing against you?' But Jesus remained silent and gave no answer." "'Aren't you going to answer?'" Pilate echoed a little later. "'See how many things they are accusing you of!' But

Jesus still made no reply, and Pilate was amazed" (Mark 14:55, 60; 15:4-5).

HOW GREAT IS THE DAMAGE?

The ninth commandment highlights just one aspect of "tongue abuse"—telling lies in court. But once that small stone is dropped into the pool of life, the ripples spread through a wide range of human relationships. According to the Bible, falsehood poisons social relationships, personal relationships, and relationships with God. It even ruins the consistency of a person's inner relationship with himself or herself.

Social relationships. The Old Testament prophets slammed those who perverted the course of justice by lies, bribes, tricks, or favoritism. Crooked judges, double-dealing businessmen, devious politicians, and any others who were "economical with the truth" came under their heavy hammer.

If those prophets lived today, would they have anything to say to us? Well, they could hardly have stayed silent for long.

British people, especially those who travel widely, have always secretly congratulated themselves on their legal system. British judges are never corrupt, and British policemen are just wonderful. Or so we thought.

That illusion has been blown sky-high by recent events in England. The convictions of ten Irish people, most of whom have spent the last decade in jail, have been questioned. Drop the names of the "Birmingham Six" or the "Guildford Four" into any casual conversation in a police canteen or a judges' club at present, and the air is likely to turn very frosty indeed. With the discovery that evidence had been fabricated and confessions extracted from prisoners by threats, a special police unit has been disbanded and the courts' reputation for fair play has been badly tarnished.

Those who were wrongfully convicted and jailed have investigative journalists to thank for their release. But the press can be equally guilty of dishonesty. My honeymoon hotel in the Lake District happened to be the headquarters of the local mountain rescue service. While we were there, a student who had a vacation job in the hotel kitchen disappeared on his day off. The rescue service was mobilized, and the press arrived to take photographs. When reporters were told that the rescue party was far too busy to pose for pictures, a group of hotel guests was rounded up to face the camera instead. They were quite surprised to find themselves featured as intrepid mountain rescuers in that newspaper the following day.

To be fair, it is virtually impossible for reporting to be strictly accurate and unbiased. C. P. Scott, when he was editor of the *Guardian,* wrote, "Comment is free: facts are sacred." That was a famous and noble sentiment, but most media people today would regard it as totally unrealistic. Comment will always enter into the way news is presented. An invading army will be either "liberators" or "aggressors," depending whose side you (and your readers) are on.

Politicians are past masters at massaging the truth. As Stuart Blanch puts it, "We live in a world now where the lie is not just a hasty response to an unwelcome situation, but an instrument of policy." Statistics are manipulated to support desired policies. At election time, the propaganda machines set out their special selection of facts, and the "dirty tricks brigade" gets to work trashing the opposition.

Blanch, writing in 1981, reminds his readers of George Orwell's Ministry of Truth with its three party slogans: "War Is Peace. Freedom Is Slavery. Ignorance Is Strength." Living on the other side of 1984, it is not so hard to believe in those slogans today. Isaiah knew politicians who bragged, "When an overwhelming scourge sweeps by, it cannot touch us, for we have made a lie our refuge and falsehood our hiding place"

(Isaiah 28:15). They have traveled well down
the centuries.

Personal relationships. When we turn from the
public to the private sector, the modern picture
is just as gloomy and just as biblical.

Paul warned the Christian groups he knew
against two kinds of falsehood-dealers. Either
could be relied on to ruin the harmony of a
church and spoil the most beautiful of relationships. There was the "gossip" and the "slanderer" (see, for example, Romans 1:29-30 and
2 Corinthians 12:20).

Paul's own language is more vivid than ours.
The gossip is literally a "whisperer." And the
slanderer is someone who "talks someone
down."

Put that way, it is easy to identify these characters in most churches. Christian whisperers
spread news faster than any professional agency.
The first thing my wife and I did after getting
engaged was to attend an evening service in our
local church. She was up at the front, singing in
the choir. I was in a seat at the back. When the
service started, no one knew about our engage-
ment. By the time it finished, people were whis-
pering their congratulations to me. The ring had
been spotted, and the good news had traveled
the length of the building while everyone should

really have been singing and praying instead of
passing on messages.

That was nice. But Christian gossip is not
always so pleasant. Rumors, many of them completely false, ruin reputations as they spread.
Those who pass them on express their pious
shock ("Please pray for_____. Didn't
you know . . . ?"), but gloating enjoyment is
only just beneath the surface.

I think of a vicar I know. A visitor in the vicar-
age thought she overheard something that put
him in a bad light. In the following days she
went systematically through the village, whisper-
ing the news from door to door. The result was
that nobody spoke to the vicar for six weeks. He,
of course, was in a no-win situation. If he followed her around the houses to put the record
straight, there would have been dark mutterings
of "no smoke without fire." If he stayed silent,
people would conclude that there must be a case
to answer.

As we all know, it is quite possible to "talk
someone down" without being so obvious about
it. When something damaging is said about
somebody else, a quiet smile and shrug of the
shoulders can be as eloquent as a long speech.
And a suggestive question can poison the best-
motivated action. That was Satan's tactic in the
face of Job's brilliant life-style. "Does Job fear

God for nothing?" he insinuated (Job 1:9). There have been many replays of that devilish little trick since.

Why do we do it? There are many reasons, if we are honest enough to admit to them. We may be afraid, as Adam was when he pointed the finger at Eve. We may be jealous. Those who procured Jesus' execution on false evidence were certainly envious of his growing influence at their expense. Pride may come into the picture, too. Talking someone down may seem the only way of climbing the rungs of the social ladder yourself.

And sometimes (let's be frank) we do it simply because we rather enjoy it. Just like the most avid readers of the weekly exposures in the popular Sunday newspapers, we sometimes catch ourselves taking "delight in lies" (Psalm 62:4).

Whatever the motives may be, the Bible condemns slander and gossip in the strongest terms. "Do not spread false reports," warns the Old Testament law (Exodus 23:1). "I tell you," Jesus adds, "that men will have to give account on the day of judgment for every careless word they have spoken" (Matthew 12:36).

TELLING LIES ABOUT GOD AND YOURSELF

Perhaps the most incredible thing about Jesus

Christ was the way he put his reputation into the hands of his disciples. "You will be my witnesses," he told them (Acts 1:8).

Perhaps that was why he did not surround himself with "idea people." No judge likes a witness who prefers his own theories about an incident to what he actually saw and heard. John the apostle would have scored highly in that respect. He stuck closely to the facts. "That which was from the beginning," he wrote, "which we have *heard,* which we have *seen* with our eyes, which we have *looked at* and our hands have *touched*—this we proclaim concerning the Word of life" (1 John 1:1, emphasis mine).

In that light, it is all the more ironic to read George Bernard Shaw's criticism of Christianity. "The trouble with Christ," he wrote, "was that he had disciples."

As a teacher in a theological college, I know what Shaw meant only too well. Our college library shelves are full of books that suggest and speculate and theorize and argue about the life and teaching of Jesus. Their authors would not pass the witness-box test. Some of them, to be honest, would fail the orthodoxy test as well. The witness they give, such as it is, is false.

The Bible has no time at all for people who set themselves up as God's spokesmen and then deliver false messages in his name. "'I am

against the prophets who wag their own tongues
. . . ,' declares the LORD. 'They . . . lead my
people astray with their reckless lies, yet I did
not send or appoint them'" (Jeremiah 23:31-32).

Telling lies about oneself is only marginally
better than lying about God. Jesus often put his
finger on that painful spot in our human
makeup. He called it *hypocrisy,* which means
acting a part.

Sometimes, we can turn life into a game of
charades. We do our best to hide the people we
really are behind the people we pretend to be.
We do not simply *tell* lies. We *become* lies. And
we may get into our parts so thoroughly that we
end up by actually believing in the false characters we have created.

Pride is usually responsible. Like the alco-
holic who refuses to believe she has a problem
with drink, we prefer to hide the ugly side of our
natures. We may even fool others as we go
through the motions of living the kind of life
that ought to win God's seal of approval. But we
cannot deceive *him.* As John puts it, "If we
claim to have fellowship with him yet walk in
the darkness, we lie and do not live by the truth"
(1 John 1:6).

John goes on, "If we claim to be without sin,
we deceive ourselves and the truth is not in
us. . . . If we claim we have not sinned, we make

him out to be a liar and his word has no place in our lives" (1:8, 10). The ultimate self-lie, which carries its own death sentence, is to pretend that we have no need of a Savior.

GOD AND THE DEVIL

"Whispered insinuations are the rhetoric of the devil," wrote Goethe. Jesus agreed. Lying is the devil's native language, the Lord taught his disciples. "When he lies, he speaks his native language, for he is a liar and the father of lies" (John 8:44).

The Bible makes that absolutely plain. When creation was in its infancy, it was the devil who misrepresented God to man with a suggestive question ("Did God *really* say that?"), followed up swiftly by a provocative answer ("Well, he *would* say that, wouldn't he!"). And when the Christian church was in its infancy, it was the devil again who ruined everything by coaxing a man and his wife to lie (see Acts 5:1-11). Even the devil's name expresses his character. The word *devil* means "slanderer." "He that raises a slander carries the devil in his tongue," commented Thomas Watson, "and he that receives it, carries the devil in his ear."

God, on the other hand, is constitutionally incapable of lying. As Paul wrote to Titus, telling lies is one of the few things God just cannot do (see Titus 1:2). There is no gap of credibility between his words and his thoughts, or between his thoughts and his nature. God the Trinity— Father, Son, and Holy Spirit—*is* truth (see John 14:6, 17). That is why we can trust his word without reservation and pin our hopes with complete confidence on his promises.

This is the first and greatest reason why Christians are still bound to obey the ninth commandment. Not to do so would be to put them on the wrong side in the war of the universe. Bearing false witness is something that the devil loves and that God hates. The book of Proverbs lists "six things the LORD hates, seven that are detestable to him." And two of the seven are "a lying tongue" and "a false witness who pours out lies" (Proverbs 6:16-19).

CAN LYING EVER BE RIGHT?

Nothing God hates can be *good*. That goes without saying. But in this sin-soaked world, as we were thinking in chapter 8, we sometimes do not have a choice between something good and something bad. There are times when the only choice we have is between staying in the frying pan or jumping into the fire. All the options available are bad—but we have to do something. And on those occasions the best we can do is to pick the least bad alternative.

That, I believe, is why the Bible approves of lying on rare occasions. The best-known example is that of Rahab. We met her in chapter 8, too. Rahab worked as a prostitute in Jericho. One day two men knocked at her door. They were Israelite spies, looking for shelter, not sex. At great risk to herself, Rahab took them in and hid them. When the secret police arrived and asked her to hand her guests over, she told them the men had gone.

It was a blatant lie, but it saved lives (including hers). And in the New Testament, James brackets Rahab with Abraham as two shining examples of people who were willing to put their faith in God into practice (see James 2:20-26).

All lies, including Rahab's, displease God. But if it comes to a straight choice between telling a lie or forfeiting a life, few of us would doubt what God wants us to do. In a situation like that, the lie is less bad than the alternative.

I once found myself in exactly this dilemma. A soldier's wife knocked on our door late at night, asking for refuge. Half an hour later, her husband arrived. He was in a rage, half-drunk. "Is my wife in here?" he thundered. There was no time to call the police and no way I could stop a more powerful man in his tracks. So, for the woman's sake, I lied.

Looking back, I am not proud of my lie. I could never call it "good" or even "white." But I still think it was the least bad thing I could have done in the circumstances.

Can we justify any other kind of deception? Most of us, I guess, reckon that God would not blame us for deceiving an enemy. When my wife and I went to church last Sunday evening, we deliberately left some lights on to fool any would-be burglar into believing that there was somebody at home. And few Englishmen would condemn their government in the Second World War for massing cardboard aircraft in East Anglia in order to muddle Hitler's invasion strategy. "In wartime," said Winston Churchill, "truth is so precious that she should always be attended by a bodyguard of lies." Some people, we might add, have actually forfeited their right to our truthfulness.

But that is the point where we have to draw back a step. All deception is bad. Even when telling a lie is the least bad thing to do, there is still a moral price to pay. Who am I to decide who is worthy of my honesty—and how can I expect the victim of my last "justified" lie ever to trust me again? Even my "loving lie" for the soldier's wife will never work again, because I can never again assume that her husband will believe anything I say.

SILENCE CAN BE GOLDEN

What should I do when I hear something nasty about someone else? It might be true! Does obedience to the ninth commandment mean that I should always tell the whole truth, whatever the consequences?

The Bible does not draw that conclusion. One of the reasons why the book of Proverbs condemns gossip is because it breaks confidences (see Proverbs 11:13; 20:19). Keeping a disruptive piece of news under wraps may be the best way of making peace. Publishing it in the name of the truth may well have the opposite effect. "Without wood a fire goes out," comments Proverbs; "without gossip a quarrel dies down. As charcoal to embers and as wood to fire, so is a quarrelsome man for kindling strife" (26:20-21).

Jesus and Paul echo the same principle in the New Testament. When something serious happens to disrupt a group of believers, Jesus taught his disciples, the main objective must be to limit the damage. Normally, that will mean limiting the spread of the damaging information. If the problem can be sorted out between the people concerned, no one else need ever know. If it cannot be resolved as easily as that, as few other people as possible should be informed. And, adds Paul, if the end result is a lawsuit, with the investigating reporters scribbling madly in the press gallery, defeat for the gospel is certain whichever way the verdict goes (see Matthew 18:15-17; 1 Corinthians 6:1-8).

On a lighter note, a woman was talking to me at my front gate. Her little daughter peered at me curiously through the bars. "Hasn't that man got big ears?" she suddenly asked her mom. I was not offended. After all, it was true. But Mother went deep pink with embarrassment because I *might* have minded.

The ninth commandment does not whitewash rudeness by encouraging us to speak our minds at all times. I think of a well-known evangelist who rebuked the church's music director from the pulpit for choosing the wrong hymn at the end of the service. He may have been right. He was certainly entitled to his opinion. But he had no need to humiliate somebody else by going public.

Telling the truth (as we see it) is a good thing to do. But any good action is spoiled when it is badly motivated. I know to my hurt that I can tell the truth out of spite or jealousy. If I do that, I must not hide behind the smoke screen of the ninth commandment to excuse myself. The commandment's sting is in its tail, when it warns me not to act against my neighbor.

TRUTH IN LOVE
Jesus taught that loving our neighbors is a mark

of Christian discipleship. And it is love that provides the antidote to the spiteful, malicious use of the tongue that the ninth commandment condemns. Fear, envy, and pride conspire against the neighbor. Love, writes Paul, "does not delight in evil but rejoices with the truth" (1 Corinthians 13:6). Commenting on that verse centuries ago, Thomas Watson wrote, "Love is a well-wisher, and it is rare to speak ill of him we wish well to. . . . Love is the hinderer of slander."

When I was ordained, I had the good fortune to work with a vicar who taught me (by example, not by words) how to love. Eric Galpin was practical and uncomplicated in his loving. When he visited a housebound lady, he would get the coal in (yes, that dates us!) before he read to her from the Bible. I knew a lonely old man who used to get a regular shave from the vicar—and then a prayer. Eric was not a great administrator, and he did not like chairing meetings very much. But nobody minded, because everyone knew how genuinely he valued and cared for them. And during my three years with him, *I never heard him malign a soul.*

Some would dismiss that kind of thing as naivete. To me it was Christlikeness, and extraordinarily attractive. That man had no need to "talk people down" in order to look big. And no one "talked down" other people when they were with him, because any malicious gossip would simply have bounced back. To use Robert Schuller's vivid expression, there was no loop-hole in his handshake.

"Love always protects, always trusts," Paul goes on in 1 Corinthians 13. Slander threatens, but love stands up to protect the one who is maligned by filling in the other half of the half-truth—as Jonathan stood up for David in front of Saul (see 1 Samuel 19:4-5). Gossip breaks trust (because you cannot trust a gossiping friend with a confidence), but love cements the cracks in a vulnerable relationship and makes it stronger.

So, writes Paul in two of his other letters, "Do not lie to each other, since you have taken off your old self with its practices and have put on the new self, which is being renewed in knowl-edge in the image of its Creator" (Colossians 3:9-10). "Instead, speaking the truth in love, we will in all things grow up into him who is the Head, that is, Christ" (Ephesians 4:15).

We would be lost without words. But our tongues can do damage out of all proportion to their size. They can mislead nations, ruin friend-ships, and feed hypocrisy. That is the spiritual health warning that the ninth commandment delivers.

A Christian's words should express love for

others, not damage them. So if we are really serious about growing up into Christian maturity, we shall make sure that our tongues are used wisely to reinforce those precious relationships that the "father of lies" is out to destroy.

TO THINK AND TALK ABOUT

1. Can you think of events in your own experience that bear out the truth of James's teaching about the power of words?

2. Politics, the press, and other social institutions are all too often found to have been "economical with the truth." Is there any way we can influence things for the better?

3. How can Christians sometimes be guilty of harmful gossip under the guise of piety? Why do we do it?

4. How honest and accurate are we as witnesses about God and our relationship with him?

5. What is "the first and greatest reason why Christians are still bound to obey the ninth commandment"?

6. Can lying ever be right?

7. Can telling the whole truth ever be wrong?

TWELVE
Life's Underworld: The Tenth Commandment

You shall not covet your neighbor's house. You shall not covet your neighbor's wife, or his manservant or maidservant, his ox or donkey, or anything that belongs to your neighbor. (Exodus 20:17)

I like gardening. That sets me apart from most of my friends, who hate it. Some of them would concrete over their window boxes, given half a chance.

Why do I like gardening? Probably, if I am honest, because I relish a battle. I am the kind of gardener who prefers to tame a wilderness than to pick half a dozen microscopic weeds out of an otherwise perfect flower border.

I do not always win my battles. In the air, I usually come out the victor. If the ladybugs do

241

not oblige, a spray will take care of the aphids. At ground level, it is rather more difficult. The little blue pellets pick off most of the slugs, though I am convinced that some of them actually thrive on the bait that is meant to poison them.

It is below the ground that the enemy wins most of the contests. Some years I have watched unbelievingly while a whole row of lettuce has wilted from end to end in the course of two weeks. Eelworms, wireworms, and all other kinds of subterranean bugs munch away at the roots of my precious plants while I look on in frustrated impotence.

In a way, keeping the Ten Commandments is a similar kind of campaign. Keeping any of them is a fight, but some battles are easier to win than others.

In case you have not noticed, the contests have been getting tougher. Commandments six, seven, and eight are all about *actions*. Most of us do not find laws like these desperately hard to keep. With a little care, it is possible to live a full life without stealing, murdering, or committing adultery.

The ninth commandment is rather more difficult. It takes us on from deeds to *words,* and the tongue is notoriously hard to control. All the same, taking the commandment in its narrowest sense, many of us manage to avoid bearing false witness against our neighbors for most of the time.

It is the tenth that delivers the knockout blow. "You shall not covet" takes us into a completely new world, the underground world of *thoughts, desires, and feelings*. And in that area of life, the inner private sector that we do not allow others to penetrate, very few of us indeed can put our hands on our hearts and claim to be winners.

MOVING THE GOALPOSTS

To change the word picture, it is almost as though God has shifted the goalposts in the final period of the game. Up to this point, it has at least been clear what the Ten Commandments are. They are a set of laws, telling us to do and say (or to stop doing and saying) certain kinds of things. Anyone with eyes, ears, and spare time could walk through life behind us and ring a loud bell whenever he saw or heard us transgressing.

Once we get into attitudes, thoughts, and feelings, however, we are in an entirely different ball game. A passing policeman could arrest me if I tossed a brick through the window of a shop and ran off with a video recorder. But if I simply stared at the video with covetous eyes, he could not lay a finger on me. Things like covetousness, envy, and greed are strictly beyond the reach of law altogether.

A strange law. So what is a "law" against covetousness doing in the Ten Commandments? Scholars have asked that question for years. Some have come to the conclusion that the tenth commandment, to be consistent with the other nine, must really be about actions. Perhaps, they suggest, it is an umbrella expression that covers the inward and outward motions of wanting and taking. So it would outlaw my failure to *control* my greed when I threw the brick at the shop window.

That is certainly a tidy suggestion. But it will not do. The Hebrew word (*hamad*) takes us below the surface of activity to the motives that inspire it. There is, of course, a close connection between desires and deeds, but there is also an important cause-and-effect difference between the two.

The Old Testament prophet Micah has some sharp words for "those who plan iniquity . . . who plot evil on their beds!" "At morning's light," he goes on, "they carry it out because it is in their power to do it. They covet fields and seize them, and houses, and take them" (Micah 2:1-2). Would Micah have stifled his criticism, perhaps, if the sleepless night had not been followed by action in the morning? Surely not. The coveting itself was wrong, even if the power to do something about it was missing.

The roots of behavior. This is very much in line with Jesus' teaching. He insisted on taking his disciples beneath the surface world of deeds and words (where the Pharisees were the specialists) to the hidden depths of thoughts and feelings. Bad deeds, he taught them, have their roots in evil desires. "For from within, out of men's hearts, come evil thoughts, sexual immorality, theft, murder, adultery, greed, malice, deceit, lewdness, envy, slander, arrogance and folly. All these evils come from *inside*" (Mark 7:21-23, emphasis mine).

There are clear echoes of the Ten Commandments in that little list. And when Jesus dealt with the commandments separately, he once again insisted that the private, below-the-surface sphere of desires and attitudes is as important as the actions that might land an offender in court. What about those thoughts that pass through Mr. A's mind as he watches his next-door neighbor's pretty wife and mentally undresses her in the privacy of his bedroom? He would never actually commit adultery with her, any more than he would dare to murder Mr. B who treats her so badly—but the murderous thoughts are there in his mind all the same, along with the lust. He has, in fact, already "committed adultery with her in his heart," said Jesus (see Matthew 5:21-22, 27-28).

Real-life stories from the Old Testament illustrate just how tiny the gap between thought and action can be. In an off-guard moment, King David was wandering around the palace roof when he caught sight of a beautiful woman taking an open-air bath. He wanted her badly. It made no difference when he found out she was married. He meant to have her all the same. By the time he had succeeded in making her his own wife, he had stolen, murdered, and committed adultery along the way. Commandments six, seven, and eight had bitten the dust, along with number ten.

Years later, King Ahab did no better. He looked out of his window and saw a vineyard. What a fine vegetable garden that would make for me, he thought—so well situated and convenient. But Naboth, the owner, was not selling. So Ahab sulked. He went to bed and would not come down for dinner. In the end his wife lent a hand. Ahab got his vegetable garden, but only after Naboth had been convicted on a false charge and had been killed. A breach in the tenth commandment had brought down three others with it.

Desires, good and bad. The tenth commandment does not say, "You shall not *desire.*" To do
that would be unrealistic.

Desire is the driving force of life. We would
die without a healthy appetite for food. Mankind
would perish if the sex drive did not stimulate
couples to start babies.

Healthy ambition. Ambition can be healthy,
too. My next-door neighbors, Dick and Jen, are
better gardeners than I am. I really want my garden to look as nice as theirs. It is not envy or
jealousy or a desire to "keep up with the
Joneses" that drives me on. It is just that when I
look over the fence, I see something attractive
that I would love to extend from their little patch
to mine. So when Dick gets to work on his
beech hedge, I am stimulated to get going on my
scruffy conifers. The tenth commandment does
not ban that kind of desire.

The Bible is full of examples of thoroughly
legitimate desires. Just before the Last Supper,
Jesus told his disciples, "I have eagerly desired
to eat this Passover with you before I suffer"
(Luke 22:15). Paul said he strained for progress
in his Christian discipleship with the same fer-
vor that an Olympic athlete strives for gold. His
longing for his Christian friends to grow in their
faith hurt him as much, he wrote, as any wom-

an's painful longing to bear a child in the maternity unit (see Philippians 3:14; Galatians 4:19).

"Eagerly desire the greater gifts," Paul told some church members whose ambitions needed re-aiming. "If anyone sets his heart on being a bishop (or an overseer)," he explained to others, "he desires a noble task" (1 Corinthians 12:31; 1 Timothy 3:1).

So the elimination of desire does not feature in the Christian manifesto. But when does legitimate desire become illegitimate covetousness?

Unhealthy grasping. The boundary between the two does get fuzzy at times. The word Paul uses for "setting your heart on" becoming a church leader actually means "stretching out your hand." There is an important difference, as we know only too well, between stretching out to grasp a job that will drain your energy in costly service and grabbing at a position that will bring you status and privilege. Only God knows whether the motives of any candidate for church leadership are pure or mixed.

Covetousness is stretching out your hand for something (or someone) that is beyond your reach, straining after a thing (or a person) that God does not want you to have.

The thing in question may be in a shop window. You want it badly, but you know you cannot or should not afford it. Or it may belong to someone else. In that case, you may be able to get it (or him or her), but only by using trickery or force.

It may be, of course, that no amount of money and pressure will ever get you the thing you want most. It might be marriage, perhaps (but not to the neighbor's husband), or a reputation for kindness (but not the job of chairing the local charity project).

Covetousness is self-centered. It stops you from appreciating what you have got. It eats you up with desire for what other people have got. And it preoccupies you with the gap between the two.

THE DIMENSIONS OF COVETOUSNESS

What does covetousness look like when you take the wrappers off? Well, it is certainly very ugly, and it stains every corner of human experience.

Envy and violence. At the personal level, whether it is a thing or a person that is the object of the greedy stare, covetousness breeds envy and violence.

James sets this out with typical vividness. "What causes fights and quarrels among you?" he asks. "Don't they come from your desires that battle within you? You want something but don't get it. You kill and covet, but you cannot have what you want. You quarrel and fight" (James 4:1-2).

The word James uses for "covet" there has overtones of jealousy. It is not just that I want something badly. I want it because someone else has got it.

I was quite content with my aging Ford until my colleague bought his sparkling new BMW. How did he find the cash to buy that, I wonder? And why should he have a BMW while I muddle along with my old Escort? I *need* a BMW. God knows I do. And if I can't have one this month, I hope the oil pan falls off his, halfway up the expressway and miles from the nearest service area.

At this level, covetousness can sometimes hide behind a mask of respectability. The apostles did not "put on a mask to cover up greed," Paul writes (1 Thessalonians 2:5). What did he mean?

Well, in his searching exposure of wrong attitudes to possessions, Jesus identified two masks that can disguise greed. They are so different that it is hard to believe they can fit the same face, but they do.

The first is *provision* for the future. Jesus told a story about a rich farmer who took early retirement. He wanted enough to see out his days in the comfort to which he was accustomed, so he hoarded everything he had. He was an excellent conservationist. So where did he go wrong? "He stored up things for himself," said Jesus. His forward-looking approach to life was basically selfish.

The label on the second mask is *anxiety* for the future. Jesus gently reproached people who, unlike the wealthy farmer, had nothing at all to hoard. They spent all their todays worrying about where their tomorrows' essentials would come from. In their own way, they were being just as self-centered. Poverty can stimulate envy just as easily as wealth. Instead of "setting their heart" on food, drink, and clothes, poor people must pin their hopes on God's provision, Jesus said, if they are not to break the tenth commandment. "Watch out!" he warned both the hoarders and the anxiety ridden. "Be on your guard against all kinds of greed" (see Luke 12:13-34).

EXPLOITATION AND UNREST

At the socioeconomic level, covetousness breeds exploitation and unrest.

Whatever the virtues of capitalism, it is undeniably a system that breeds and encourages covetous people. The wheels of industry turn only when men and women can be persuaded to discard their old things and buy new at regular intervals.

The arch-persuaders are, of course, the advertisers. The advertising industry stimulates the itch to possess and then offers goods to soothe the irritation—for the time being. It is unfair to accuse advertisers of creating greed in the first place. They merely reflect and focus the desires that are already there in the hearts and minds of the consumers. But the total effect, when persuasion eclipses information, is to reinforce the self-centered, restless approach to life that the tenth commandment condemns.

Capitalism thrives on competition. There is a healthy side to that, too. But when the competitive spirit leads multinationals to give profit priority over the welfare of their work force, and sets one group of working people against another in order to protect its profit-and-loss statement, the tenth commandment cries out for an Old Testament prophet to update its application.

Stuart Blanch tells a story to show how insidiously the profit motive can poison our social life. In one town, a narrowing in a busy road produced a regular crop of accidents. So the borough council discussed a proposal to widen the road. It seemed logical enough, but the scheme gained the votes it needed only when someone showed that the cost of the roadwork would be less than the expense of providing extra facilities at the hospital and enlarging the mortuary to cope with the accident victims. The right decision was made—but for quite the wrong reasons.

Covetous prayers. Even at the religious level, covetousness can rear its ugly head. Peter writes scornfully about false preachers who exploit their congregations with attractively made-up stories, in order to fill the collection bags (see 2 Peter 2:3). And we have all heard arm-twisting prayers that coax God to provide the things people want but cannot get without divine intervention.

It sometimes seems that people only see a mirror image of the word *God* when they pray. The Creator to whom the whole universe belongs is pressed into service as a guard dog to protect this or that little pile of human goodies. When that happens, the Good Shepherd has become little more than a German shepherd in the eyes of his covetous worshipers.

A BLIND ALLEY

The Bible is a very practical book. The worst thing about covetousness, Scripture says, is that when you get to the bottom line it does not produce what it has promised.

There are two reasons for that.

No satisfaction. The first is that the hunger of a covetous person can never be satisfied. Ecclesiastes puts it very clearly: "Whoever loves money never has money enough; whoever loves wealth is never satisfied with his income." And he adds, "This too is meaningless" (Ecclesiastes 5:10).

Coveting is like drug taking. Lasting satisfaction always eludes you. You have to increase the dose constantly just to maintain the same temporary effect. The covetous man would always want someone else's wife, even if the world were overpopulated with women. The covetous woman will always shout for more, even when her stomach is full to bursting from the last big meal.

Contrast the lasting satisfaction I can give you, promised Jesus. "Whoever drinks the water I give him will never thirst. Indeed, the water I give him will become in him a spring of water welling up to eternal life" (John 4:14).

No permanence. The second reason why covetousness cannot honor its promises is that the goods it produces do not last. This time it is John, not Jesus, who draws the contrast: "The world and its desires pass away, but the man who does the will of God lives forever" (1 John 2:17).

As usual, it is James who paints the most vivid picture. "Now listen, you rich people," he

writes, "weep and wail because of the misery
that is coming upon you. Your wealth has rotted,
and moths have eaten your clothes. Your gold
and silver are corroded" (James 5:1-3).

In James's world, wealth was measured in
three ways: valuable foodstuffs, costly garments,
and precious metals. These were the major desir-
ables the covetous person would try to amass,
and James lumps all three together to show the
sheer stupidity of hoarding things that do not
last. The caviar in the freezer is already becoming tainted. Put your ear to the wardrobe door
and you will hear the moths chewing the
designer labels off your most precious clothes.
Even the stainless steel cutlery is growing mil-
dew. In the light of eternity and the certain prospect of God's judgment, the commodities with
the longest guarantees will surely disintegrate.

No progress or happiness. The shadow side of
devoting life to the collection of material desir-
ables in the here and now is that spiritual development will be stunted. In Jesus' famous story
about the sower and the soil, the thorns that
choke the growing plant and make it unfruitful
are "worries of this life and the deceitfulness of
wealth" (Matthew 13:22). "You may as well bid
an elephant fly in the air as a covetous man live
by faith," comments Thomas Watson.

Ultimately, covetousness rests on the dogma that happiness lies in getting what you have not yet got. But those who embrace this philosophy of life find themselves on a collision course with Jesus. "A man's life does not consist in the abundance of his possessions," he warned his disciples (Luke 12:15). True happiness results from serving God, not from an endless chase for things that neither satisfy nor last.

LOVE, NOT COVET
The tenth commandment is radically different from the rest. Or is it? It is, in fact, really a recall to the first. This is actually where we came in.

Loving God. The first commandment demands total loyalty to the Lord. We must put him first, ahead of all other competitors for the control center of our lives. The tenth echoes that. If the Lord is to be completely in charge of my life, the desires that drive me from the inside must come under his control, just as firmly as my outward actions and words.

Covetousness, Paul pointed out, is only idolatry in thin disguise (see Ephesians 5:5). The thing that I covet dominates me. My craving for it fills all my horizons. It holds my heart captive. If money is my goal, I can spell that word with a

capital *M* because it has become my god. And if
all that sounds highly dramatic and unrealistic, it
is only a clear echo of what Jesus himself
taught. "Where your treasure is," he told his disciples, "there your heart will be also. . . . No one
can serve two masters. Either he will hate the
one and love the other, or he will be devoted to
the one and despise the other. You cannot serve
both God and Money" (Matthew 6:21, 24).

Did you notice the word *love* creeping into
that stark statement? The languages of love and
law seem poles apart, but this is where they
meet. When, in answer to a lawyer's question,
Jesus said that the greatest *commandment* was to
love the Lord (see Mark 12:28-30), he was not
setting law and love on a collision course. He
was simply showing how they relate.

When I covet something, it becomes the
object of my love. If that "something" is money
(or something money can buy), I am on a trail to
disaster. This is the Bible's clear message. "The
love of money," Paul warned, "is a root of all
kinds of evil" (1 Timothy 6:10). The answer is
to transfer my affections. "Keep your lives free
from the love of money and be content with
what you have, because God has said, 'Never
will I leave you; never will I forsake you'"
(Hebrews 13:5).

Here is the antidote to covetousness. Coveting

is all to do with my will and my feelings. So is love. If I love God with all my heart and with all my soul and with all my mind and with all my strength, I will trust him. It is crazy for me to gaze with longing through retailers' shop windows when I have free access to the Wholesale Supply Center of the universe. The God who feeds the birds and gilds the lilies will see to it that I have the food and clothes I need.

That is realism, not naivete. And any gap between my needs and my wants will have to be closed by an adjustment to my loving trust. Then, free from coveting, I will be able to say with Paul, "I have learned the secret of being content in any and every situation, whether well fed or hungry, whether living in plenty or in want. I can do everything through him who gives me strength" (Philippians 4:12-13).

Loving others. The tenth commandment recalls us to the first, because coveting is idolatry. But it also turns our attention to our neighbors. It is their property, after all, that is usually the object of our greed.

In sounding that note, too, this commandment anticipates the teaching of Jesus. If the most important rule of life is "Love the Lord your God," then the runner-up has to be, "Love your neighbor as yourself" (see Mark 12:31).

Once again, the Old Testament law and Jesus are in harmony. The tenth commandment takes us below the surface of life's deeds and words to the drives and desires that motivate our behavior. And love speaks that kind of language, too.

Think of someone you genuinely love. Then tune your mind to something he or she has that you would like to have yourself. Would you steal it? Would you lurk in the shadows of a subway and snatch it? Or if the "something" is physical beauty, not property, would you rape?

In a genuinely loving relationship, questions like those just do not appear on the agenda. You are more preoccupied with the loved one's good than with their goods. You may want to share, but you have no urge to snatch. Instead of that, you take every opportunity to give, and you are delighted when an expensive present gives real pleasure. Covetousness is eclipsed by generosity.

Luke tells how one man followed up Jesus' two love commandments with a supplementary question. "And who *is* my neighbor?" he asked.

It was a good question, and it drew from Jesus one of his most famous illustrations, the story of the Good Samaritan. In Jewish popular opinion, your "neighbor" was someone to whom you were related. Members of the extended family were candidates for neighbor love, as were all your fellow Jews—but not foreigners. Jesus' story smashed flat that artificial barrier. Anyone in need is your neighbor, insider or outsider, he taught. And his punch line was practical and direct: "Go and do likewise" (see Luke 10:25-37).

In chapter 1, we saw how God's law is needed to keep our lives running securely on his tracks. It is unhelpful and wrong to throw the Ten Commandments out of the window and say, "We will follow the way of love instead."

I still believe that is true. But the tenth commandment exposes the inadequacy of any laws that only deal with deeds and words. I cannot please God if I refrain from stealing my neighbor's property, yet eat my heart out with envy every time I look over his fence. Nor do I win God's approval if I never commit adultery but begrudge my best friend his beautiful wife.

In other words, law without love is as dangerously unbalanced as love without law. We certainly need law to provide love with sturdy backbone. But we also need love to provide law with depth and warmth.

TO THINK AND TALK ABOUT

1. Given that coveting is something that we do in the privacy of our own minds, does it matter whether we keep this commandment or not? Why?

2. What is the difference between healthy desire and coveting?

3. How does coveting poison (a) personal relationships, (b) social structures and decisions, and (c) even our spiritual lives?

4. Do you agree that coveting can never lead to satisfaction? Why?

5. Why does the author call love for God and others "the antidote to covetousness"?

6. What do you most desire right now? Is it a legitimate desire? If it is coveting, how can you deal with it?

CONCLUSION

THIRTEEN
Power to Obey

What do you do when you have broken the law—and been found out?

One of my students, a lively extrovert from East London, parked on a double yellow line one day while he paid a brief visit to the bank. When he got back to the car, he found a police-woman taking the license number.

"What are you doing that for?" he asked in wide-eyed innocence.

"You're illegally parked," she replied. "I'm going to give you a ticket."

Ray took a look at her face. "You can't do that," he protested. "I'm black!"

"Oh yes I can," she said with a smile.

He had a closer look and spotted a cross on a chain around her neck. "But you *can't* do it. You're a Christian, and so am I!"

"You're right," she said, "I am a Christian. But you've broken the parking regulations so you're going to get a ticket—and that's that."

"OK," he replied, resigned to the inevitable. "So why don't you come to college for lunch and meet my friends?"

She did, and she has been a welcome visitor ever since.

Ray's brush with the law, his unsuccessful attempts to evade the consequences, his helpless resignation, and his success in making a friend out of the policewoman, all reflect (though not exactly, of course) our own reactions when we break one or more of the Ten Commandments. Protests of innocence give way to a sense of resignation. And then, if we are Christians, we make the exciting discovery that we can enter into an enriching, dynamic relationship with the Lord whose law we have broken.

As we finish our study of the Ten Commandments, that process is worth exploring in a little more detail.

HELPLESSNESS

Faced by the uncomfortable fact that we break God's law, we sometimes resort to evasion.

"Well, no one's perfect!" is a popular defense. I met a variation of that one day when a lady I was visiting told me cheerfully, "When I meet my Maker, my scales will balance."

If you think of the Ten Commandments as an exam paper, that is a perfectly reasonable (and comforting) idea. Providing God's passing mark is 50 percent, or thereabouts, most of us will squeeze through with a little bit to spare. Our scales will balance. It would be even better, of course, if there was a heading at the top of the paper that told us that we need only attempt seven or eight out of the ten.

Paul tells us that he would have passed God's test himself on that basis. As a Pharisee, he had made a professional point of living an outwardly blameless life. He could put a personal tick beside the first nine of the Ten Commandments.

Unfortunately, the tenth proved to be the sticking point. Not only was Paul unable to put his hand on his heart and say, "I never covet," but he found that the ticks beside the other nine commandments had to be changed to crosses once his thoughts and feelings were brought into the reckoning.

Worse still, he made the alarming discovery that, without help, he could not keep God's law at all at this deeper level. In fact, horror of horrors, he recognized deep within himself a perverse longing to do and say and think the very things that the Ten Commandments forbade—

just because they forbade them. He was like a man who just *has* to walk on the grass because there is a notice telling him not to do it.

"I have the desire to do what is good, but I cannot carry it out," Paul confessed. "When I want to do good, evil is right there with me. What a wretched man I am! Who will rescue me . . . ?" (Romans 7:18, 21, 24).

Personally, I am deeply grateful to Paul for wearing his heart on his sleeve so honestly. It makes me feel more like a normal human being and less of a freak, because I share his experience of helplessness almost exactly. So, I guess, may you. When we examine our human reflections in the mirror of the Ten Commandments—taken as a whole—we do not see proud, godly successes but sad, abject failures.

The Ten Commandments themselves do nothing to help us out of this fix. They spell out God's demands very plainly, as we have seen, but they give us no help at all in discovering what to do when we fail to come up to their standard. In fact they add to our sense of helplessness.

The great German theologian, Helmut Thielicke, describes God's law as "gauze in the wound." It does not heal, but it is a constant reminder that we are hurting. He also uses the word picture of a sheepdog. As the dog makes the sheep's life uncomfortable when it strays, so the Ten Commandments are an irritant when we step out of line.

RESIGNATION

When my daughter was three, she locked me in the garden shed by mistake. Whatever she did, prompted by my shouted instructions through the door, she could not turn the key and let me out. So she trotted into the house, curled up in an armchair, and fell fast asleep until mother got home. Her antidote to helplessness was resignation.

In our more sophisticated adult ways, we can cope with failure along similar lines.

We live today in an age of moral pessimism. Levels of expectation are very low as far as human behavior is concerned. No one is really expected to live up to the Ten Commandments anymore. In fact, if a modern Paul came on the scene with the claim that he had kept nine out of the ten perfectly, we would immediately suspect him of hypocritical humbug. The old humanist dreams that selfishness, cruelty, and all other barriers to human moral progress will disappear with the advance of education seem as outdated now as halfpennies and shillings.

Strangely, though, no one is wringing his hands in despair. Our experience of moral failure causes very little distress. We prefer to retreat into our armchairs and resign ourselves to the inevitable. Regard your shortcomings as unavoidable, we are told, and they will stop bothering you. The best cure for a troubled conscience is to understand *why* you fail, and then you will stop worrying about it. *"Tout comprendre est tout pardonner,"* as the French would say.

Canon Fenton Morley captured this spirit of the age perfectly in a sermon he preached in Leeds University Church. A student had just been expelled from Oxford for immoral behavior (the last one, surely!) and the headlines were full of outrage and protest. Morley showed how even the old titles of the seven deadly sins had succumbed to the influence of conscience sedatives.

"We have turned *pride* into self-fulfillment," he said, *"envy* into insecurity, *anger* into stress, *avarice* into the pursuit of incentives, *sloth* into constitutional inertia, *gluttony* into defective metabolism, and *lust* into emotional tension."

Translated into such terms, old-fashioned sin calls for sympathetic understanding, not stern condemnation. We empathize with those who break the Ten Commandments, but we do not blame them.

The Bible does not allow us to get away with evasion tactics like these. It points us toward a more honest and satisfactory solution.

PARDON

It asks us to begin by being more realistic about ourselves. We cannot please God by keeping some of the Ten Commandments reasonably well for most of the time. His standards are higher than that. Nor can we shelve the blame for our failings on anyone or anything else. Knowing *why* we fail is not enough.

Paul was right. The tenth commandment is the killer. That is because it points the finger at the kind of people we *are,* not just at the kind of things we *do* and *say.* Measured by that standard, all human beings have to shake their heads in silent helplessness. In Alec Vidler's wise words, "The Decalogue has a terrible sting in its tail."

James helps us get the message with another of his vivid word pictures. He uses the language of conception and childbirth to illustrate the chain reaction that is set off when we break the tenth commandment: "After desire has conceived, it gives birth to sin; and sin, when it is full-grown, gives birth to death" (James 1:15). And Paul caps that with an eloquent word picture of his own. "The wages of sin is death," he writes grimly to his Christian friends in Rome (Romans 6:23).

All this sounds like very bad news. But the New Testament has some marvelously good news to drown its somber warnings. For all who are prepared to admit their helplessness, instead of evading it, there is a free pardon in Jesus Christ. Jesus died to save us from the consequences of breaking the Ten Commandments. That is the Christian Good News. In his amazing love, he took our death penalty on himself.

Without the Cross, God's law is a sentence of death. That is the final consequence of breaking it. But in the light of all that happened on the first Good Friday and Easter Day, the Ten Commandments become our signpost to life.

My home is on the outskirts of London. It never gets properly dark at night where I live. There is always an artificial glow that makes it difficult to pick out the stars. But when I get out of London to the place I love best, the countryside of West Dorset, the moon and the stars sparkle against the backdrop of a jet black sky.

The Ten Commandments are God's backdrop. Without them, we would never see our need for his pardon clearly. With them, the harsh exposure of our helplessness makes us want—really badly—the free pardon that he offers. And God never turns anyone away who comes to him in a humble, dependent frame of mind.

POWER
God's good news of pardon releases us from the

guilt of failure. It also opens up vast new potential for keeping his commandments.

Accepting God's pardon restores our good relationship with him. As they looked forward to Jesus' arrival in the world, the Old Testament prophets described that breathtaking transformation as "having a new heart." "I will give you a new heart and put a new spirit in you," the Lord promised through Ezekiel (36:26). And God echoed this prediction through Jeremiah: "I will put my law in their minds and write it on their hearts" (31:33).

Looking back on Jesus Christ's life, death, and resurrection, the New Testament writers talked in the same kind of way about "becoming a new person." Paul exclaimed, "If anyone is in Christ, he is a new creation; the old has gone, the new has come! All this is from God, who reconciled us to himself through Christ" (2 Corinthians 5:17-18).

As Christians, we are new people. That is the Bible's best news. We still need the Ten Commandments as life's signposts, but they now speak to us in a fresh way. Instead of coming at us from the outside, with an implied threat, they now speak to us from the heart, where Christ himself is alive and active. We now *want* to please God. And, to our joy, we find we actually *can*.

The New Testament tumbles over itself to

express this radical change. Each person of the Trinity is involved in charging our Christian lives with fresh potential.

God the Father welcomes us into his kingdom. Jesus' call to "enter the kingdom of God" was much more than a summons to unconditional surrender. As well as a demand for total obedience, it was an invitation to share the King's power.

The guidance and strength of the King are immediately available to those who put themselves under his rule. With his commandments as our signposts, we have the light we need to make right decisions and the strength we need to carry those decisions into practice. Living in God's kingdom spells an end to spiritual and moral helplessness.

God the Son feeds his resurrection power into our lives. "You have been raised with Christ," Paul reminds the church members at Colosse. "For you died, and your life is now hidden with Christ in God" (Colossians 3:1, 3).

As Christians we live "in Christ." He frees us to live in step with the Ten Commandments. In him we are liberated from life's destructive influences around us and from the snowball effect of our own past failures. Real freedom does not just mean being free to *do* things, but being free *not* to do them. It is here that human willpower is so pitifully weak. In Christ we can break free from all those ingrained habits of the past and pressures of the present that threaten to master our lives.

And *God the Holy Spirit* provides us with God's inner dynamic. Jesus returned "in the power of the Spirit" from his successful battle with his spiritual enemy in the desert (Luke 4:14). And it is the same Spirit who enables Christians to win the fight against those forces of human nature that prevent you from doing what you would (see Galatians 5:16-17).

The Holy Spirit transforms us by directing God's light into those murky areas of our lives that we try to hide from other people's eyes. And he provides us with the resources of love that we need to keep the Ten Commandments as Jesus summarized them. In Paul's grateful words, "God has poured out his love into our hearts by the Holy Spirit, whom he has given us" (Romans 5:5).

One of the people I most admire is Martin Hallett. Martin runs an organization called True Freedom Trust, which offers Christian advice and support to homosexuals.

A few years ago, Martin and I found ourselves on the same platform. Before the meeting started, we were both quite apprehensive as we looked around at our audience. About 90 percent of them were obviously gay activists.

I spoke first, and it very soon became obvious that the main intention of those in the hall was to disrupt the meeting. I was heckled so loudly that I very much doubt whether anyone more than two rows from the front heard a word. One guy had brought along a large, old-fashioned pulpit Bible. He amused himself during my talk by tearing out the pages, twisting them into paper balls, and throwing them at me. I confess I ducked when the binding (with its brass clasp) eventually arrived.

Pandemonium reigned. Then I sat down and Martin got to his feet. "I, too, am a homosexual," he began. Immediately there was a hush. "I was on the gay scene for ten years," he went on. Now they were really interested. "And I want to tell you that I have stopped doing it."

The silence was electric, until an unbelieving voice broke in from halfway back in the hall: "But you *can't* stop."

"I *have* stopped," Martin quietly insisted, "through the power of Jesus Christ."

There, in a nutshell, is the New Testament's postscript to the Ten Commandments. (We have already noticed, by the way, that Paul includes homosexual behavior in an updated version of the Ten Commandments—see 1 Timothy 1:9-10).